P9-DCJ-749

"In a warm, comforting, and down-to-earth voice, Beverly Berg offers powerful, heartfelt help for couples and families grappling with addiction and recovery. Grounded in the latest neuroscience and illuminated by mindfulness, her book offers practical tools and advice for lasting love and happiness. Beverly writes with charm, humor, and the bone-deep understanding that comes from someone who has been there herself. This book is a remarkable achievement, at once compelling and profound, cheerful and wise."

—**Rick Hanson, PhD**, author of *Buddha's Brain* and
Hardwiring Happiness

"*Loving Someone in Recovery* is the real deal: insightful, comprehensive, funny, and beautifully written. It's like having someone very wise walking beside you through rough terrain. And what a wonderful guide Beverly Berg is. Her knowledge comes through on every page. She speaks as a person who has been there, and as a clinician with years of experience helping real people put their lives back together. Anyone touched by a recovering person they care about needs this book. It has the power to change your life."

—**Terrence Real, MSW, LCSW**, author of *The New Rules of Marriage:
What You Need to Know to Make Marriage Work*

"With a strong understanding of addiction recovery and many years of working with couples struggling in their intimate relationships, Beverly Berg masterfully addresses the codependency that undermines the potential for a happy coupleship. While she recognizes the complexity of the challenges, she also knows the hope that comes with the possibilities. With a delightful writing style, she offers her readers concrete, do-able tools, and gives them the skills needed to create a healthy and happy relationship. This is the seminal book for couples confronted with the recovery of addiction and the age-old issue of codependency that undermines the promises."

—**Claudia Black, PhD**, author of *It Will Never Happen to Me: Changing
Course* and *Deceived: Facing Sexual Betrayal, Lies and Secrets*

"*Loving Someone in Recovery* is a groundbreaking, practical, and brilliant guide. It will give heart and support to millions in recovery and help them to learn to love wisely at last."

—**Jack Kornfield, PhD**, best-selling author of *A Path with Heart*

"Using her experiences from working with her clients, Beverly Berg has written a moving and helpful book for all couples seeking an intimate and fulfilling relationship. Through her use of specific and clear tools, the reader has available the possibility of creating intimacy, as well as tools for addressing the conflicts that occur in relationships and moving toward a greater understanding of love and commitment. In my books, *Coupleship* and *Understanding Codependency*, these are tenants of a fulfilling relationship. Berg offers a whole new dimension for growing together, and separately, in a healthy relationship. I applaud her book, *Loving Someone in Recovery*."

> —**Sharon Wegscheider-Cruse, MA**, author of *Coupleship* and *Understanding Codependency*, founder of Onsite Workshops, and family therapist www.sharonwcruse.com

"Beverly Berg touches upon some of the most sensitive and raw issues a human being can experience: the conflict, unpredictability, and 'not-knowing' of the recovery process. But she gives us a way home with kindness and counsel that help turn this into a redemptive and transformational experience. Enjoy the ride!"

> —**Tim Ryan**, United States congressman, co-chair of the House Caucus on Addiction and Recovery, and author of *A Mindful Nation*

"If you are part of a recovering couple and looking for a handbook on how to transform the quality of relationship from dysfunction to healing and connection, you've found it. Grounded in deep personal and professional experience, combined with a warm and witty sense of humor, Beverly Berg lights the path for a better future for yourself and your relationship. Stop, listen, and soak up these powerful lessons!"

> —**Elisha Goldstein, PhD**, author of *The Now Effect: How this Moment Can Change the Rest of Your Life* and coauthor of *A Mindfulness-Based Stress Reduction Workbook*

"Beverly Berg outlines the framework of a recovering couple's relationship in direct and clear ways that will bring a taste of reality to those struggling with codependence and recovery from addiction. Her descriptions of the entangled codependent relationship are clear and free from jargon; her guidance on moving into a more healthy, loving, and grounded connection are practical and to the point. A valuable guide for every couple facing the challenges of recovery."

> —**Kevin Griffin**, author of *One Breath at a Time: Buddhism and the Twelve Steps* and *A Burning Desire: Dharma God and the Path of Recovery*

"*Loving Someone in Recovery* is a pivotal book of our time for the recovering codependent. This book addresses the universal issues codependents and their addict partners struggle with after entering the world of recovery. With humor and straight-up talk, Beverly Berg, an expert in her field, provides answers to common questions and a clear path to follow. I strongly recommend this book!"

—**Gabrielle Bernstein**, author of *Spirit Junkie*

"Beverly Berg writes with deep understanding and compassion. Filled with practical advice and exercises, this book is an invaluable resource for anyone in a relationship with someone in recovery."

—**Sharon Salzberg**, author of *Real Happiness* and *Lovingkindness*

"Beverly Berg writes about secure attachment and self-care with extraordinary intelligence, warmth, wit, and compassion in a book that will absolutely change your life. On every page of this profound and deeply meaningful book, she expertly guides her readers to an essential understanding about one of the most important tenets of any relationship: how to stay separate yet connected. Her brilliant insight and understanding of couple dynamics, along with the fascinating mindfulness exercises she provides, gives readers the tools to chip away at old, negative patterns and build a new way of interacting with their partners. Whether you are in recovery or are simply seeking to incorporate healthier responses to those you love, this book will impact all of your important relationships—including those with your parents, your children, and your co-workers—in the most positive ways. If this book had been available when my mother was still alive, I'm confident that it singlehandedly would have had the power to put our relationship back on track."

—**Kathryn Stern**, novelist and author of *Another Song about the King*

"If I had been able to read *Loving Someone in Recovery* thirty-three years ago, my wife would not have had to practice her serial forgiveness quite so much, and our marriage would have been saved from a lot of pain. Beverly Berg's book is one that should be mandated for anyone who has issues of codependency and is in a committed partnership with a recovering addict. It will not only save you from unnecessary pain in your relationship, it will show you how to bring a new happiness and joy to it as well."

—**Ted Klontz, PhD**, author of *The Financial Wisdom of Ebenezer Scrooge: 5 Principles to Transform Your Relationship with Money*

"*Loving Someone in Recovery* is an excellent road map for couples to find their way back to the healthy and passionate relationship that they first envisioned. Berg's book fills an enormous void in the current addiction literature by focusing on the often neglected codependent partner, and is fast becoming an essential resource in my practice. From heroin to Häagen-Dazs, this book addresses what has truncated so many of my patients' therapeutic progress, and provides clear guidance in order to restore both their emotional and physical well-being."

> —**Louisa L. Williams, MS, DC, ND**, naturopathic doctor and author of *Radical Medicine*

"Beverly Berg's creative work with couples recovering from addiction is laced with strength, humor, compassion. Most significantly, reveals her lifelong dedication to this essential and compelling calling. Her comprehensive book, *Loving Someone in Recovery,* is a treasure chest of discoveries and insights; she shows us all how to be more true to who we really are, and in being so, to each other."

> —**Trudy Goodman**, founding teacher at InsightLA and contributing author of *Compassion and Wisdom in Psychotherapy, The Clinical Handbook of Mindfulness*, and *Mindfulness and Psychotherapy*

"I have trained, consulted, and collaborated with Beverly Berg for a number of years. I entrust clients to Beverly's capable hands frequently and without the slightest hesitation. *Loving Someone in Recovery* is a book that offers the reader a rare combination of bright, innovative, and courageous thinking, combined with empathy, humor, and practical skills for recovering couples."

> —**Ralph Bruneau, PhD, MFT**, director of Larchmont Associates and faculty professor at Antioch University, and board member of AAMFT-CALIFORNIA

"I have worked with Beverly Berg for many years, and the breadth and depth of her theoretical knowledge is truly astounding. With this knowledge, *Loving Someone in Recovery* is able to skillfully work with clients utilizing a variety of techniques. Her work with couples in recovery, in particular, is masterful."

> —**Jeffrey Gandin, MD**, diplomate of the American Board of Psychiatry and Neurology and assistant clinical professor at the Semel Institute for Neuroscience and Human Behavior at UCLA

"Recovery from addiction entails a multifaceted approach that often combines the twelve-step program and individual, family, and group therapies, as well as assessment and treatment of medical and psychiatric disorders. Beverly Berg's treatment approach to helping couples in recovery from addiction fills an important gap and is the product of her extensive clinical and personal experience. *Loving Someone in Recovery* provides practical direction in helping recovering couples and should be incorporated as a standard component of addiction treatment. Our mutual patients have significantly accrued benefit from her insights and innovations, and I recommend this book to all couples dealing with the recovery process."

> —**Harvey Sternbach, MD**, adult psychiatrist, addiction medicine specialist, clinical professor of psychiatry at UCLA, and distinguished fellow at the American Psychiatric Association

"Beverly Berg is a truly talented and gifted psychotherapist. *Loving Someone in Recovery* is gifted with a combination of compassion, an immense fund of knowledge, and extensive clinical experience. Berg is an innovator and leader in the fields of couples therapy and chemical dependency. Berg's passion for her clinical work has lead to creative breakthroughs and novel treatment approaches for improving intimacy, relationships, and quality of life for clients."

> —**Phillip J. Bowman, MD, MPH**, diplomate of the American Board of Psychiatry and Neurology and medical director at Bowman Medical Group

"Personal, relevant, and important. ... At Onsite we work daily with codependency and emotional trauma and see first-hand the dramatic effect these conditions have on relationships when untreated. Unfortunately far too many couples are torn apart by not having the tools Beverly provides in this must-read for the recovering couple. This book is an awakening to the behavioral health and addiction professional community, as this vital piece of the recovery process is often overlooked. Couples looking for more than another self-help surface guide on love and intimacy should take the time to invest in this fun, easy, and impactful resource."

> —**Miles Adcox**, CEO of Onsite Workshops

"Berg provides a perfect blueprint for newly recovering couples to navigate uncharted territory. Not only will couples learn what to expect with every stage of recovery, but mindfulness meditation tools for coping with every stage. Berg even helps couples bring mindfulness to their sex lives! So often in therapy, we come to understand the *whys?* and *how's?* of our behaviors, but to actually learn skills to cope and self-soothe is the real gold. In Berg's book, each member of the recovering couple will learn more about him or herself and will also come to understand the partner more fully. This understanding, both for the self and the partner, has the potential to bring a new kind of compassion to a once strife-ridden relationship, moving a couple from hopelessness to renewed love. I am so excited to share Berg's book with my clients!"

—**Elizabeth Hill, MFT**, addiction professional

loving someone in recovery

The Answers You Need When Your Partner Is Recovering from Addiction

BEVERLY BERG, MFT, PhD

New Harbinger Publications, Inc.

Publisher's Note

This publication is designed to provide accurate and authoritative information in regard to the subject matter covered. It is sold with the understanding that the publisher is not engaged in rendering psychological, financial, legal, or other professional services. If expert assistance or counseling is needed, the services of a competent professional should be sought.

Distributed in Canada by Raincoast Books

Copyright © 2014 by Beverly Berg
New Harbinger Publications, Inc.
5674 Shattuck Avenue
Oakland, CA 94609
www.newharbinger.com

Cover design by Amy Shoup
Acquired by Tesilya Hanauer
Edited by Ken Knabb

All Rights Reserved

Library of Congress Cataloging-in-Publication Data

Berg, Beverly.
  Loving someone in recovery : the answers you need when your partner is recovering from addiction / Beverly Berg, MFT, PhD ; foreword by Stan Tatkin.
       pages cm. -- (The New Harbinger Loving someone series)
  Summary: "In Loving Someone in Recovery, a therapist offers powerful tools for the partners of recovering addicts. Based in mindfulness, attachment theory, and neurobiol-ogy, this book will help readers sustain emotional stability in their relationships, increase effective communication, establish boundaries, and take steps to reignite intimacy. Drawn from the author's successful Conscious Couples Recovery Workshop, this book addresses the roles that both partners play in recovery, and aims to help readers rebuild trust and connection"-- Provided by publisher.
  Includes bibliographical references.
  ISBN 978-1-60882-898-2 (pbk.) -- ISBN 978-1-60882-900-2 (ebk.) -- ISBN 978-1-60882-899-9 (ebk. : pdf) 1. Recovering alcoholics--Family relationships. 2. Recovering addicts--Family relationships. I. Title.
  HV5132.B47 2014
  362.29'13--dc23
                                2013035483

Printed in the United States of America

16   15   14

10   9   8   7   6   5   4   3   2

To my husband, Brian, and my daughter, Ruby. My love for you knows no bounds. You embody my heart and soul, and I would be nowhere without either of you.

Contents

Foreword

During the late 1980s and early 1990s, I was one of the lead therapists for John Bradshaw at both LifePlus Treatment Center and Ingleside Hospital in Los Angeles, California. The matter of codependency was at the forefront of our treatment programs. During that period, Bradshaw and others broadened public awareness of addiction and codependency. The term "co-alcoholic," which had been popularized as the flip side of addiction, was reframed as "codependent." The first meeting of Co-Dependents Anonymous was held in 1986, and codependency became part of the cultural lexicon.

The recent popularity of attachment theory and neuroscience has given us additional ways to describe and approach the problem of codependency. As a couple therapist, I am especially interested in Beverly Berg's topic. Since I am one of those who have become enamored of both attachment theory and neuroscience, allow me to discuss codependency in light of the former.

From the perspective of attachment theory, if you see yourself as codependent—that is, overly invested in a partner who is currently in recovery from some form of addiction—it is quite possible you did not feel securely bonded in your earliest relationships. But fret not, because both codependency and the type of insecurity associated with it are well understood by therapists familiar with attachment theory, and are common in the Western world. So you're in good company. Saying that, however, misses the point that being in this situation makes you angry, depressed… and did I say angry?

Codependent men and women tend to bond in love relationships in a way that makes them both angry and resistant. Why? Because during their childhood, at least one of their important caregivers was preoccupied as a result of feeling overwhelmed, unsupported, and unloved by his or her own parents. Young children with a preoccupied caregiver tend to feel alternately (1) rewarded for depending on and supporting this caregiver and (2) rejected, punished, or abandoned. This inconsistency tends to make them angry, as well as suspicious of and resistant to affectionate approaches from a caregiver. Fast-forward to adult relationships with a partner "preoccupied" with addiction, and you find a familiar situation. Here you are, still anxious and insecure and prepared for the usual: "I'm not wanted and needed. I'm not important. I'm abandoned. I'm doing all the work in this relationship; this is a huge rip-off!" Welcome home to your childhood.

In love relationships, you probably see yourself as a caretaker, emotionally available to an otherwise indifferent or nonpresent partner. If your partner is an active addict, he or she knows how to feel good without you. You, on the other hand, need your partner to be present, loving, and caring so that you can feel good. Big problem here. You are left feeling ignored, abandoned, and alone, without a way to alter your own brain chemistry so that you can feel great. For that, you need your partner. Not fair. But because you are insecure and you fear abandonment, you stay in the situation, and you continue to feel angry and resentful. Even now that your partner is in recovery, he or she may be preoccupied with the recovery process. You still feel a bit unimportant because your partner is still focused on himself or herself and not you. You're waiting for some reciprocity.

In this book, you will find answers to the questions you have about how to navigate out of an anxious attachment and into a secure one. Beverly Berg intimately understands the recovering couple's struggle. Using mindfulness theory, she has outlined a systematic method to support you in recovery so that you can move from being overfocused on your partner and start—maybe for the first time in your life—to pay attention to your own self-care. From that basis, she guides you to attain the sense of mutuality, collaboration, and fair play you want and deserve in your love relationship with your recovering partner. In fact, what you want and deserve is also what your partner wants and deserves. As a couple, you should have a safe, secure, and purposeful relationship based on a set of values that serves you both. Ultimately, with increased self-care and self-focus and strong self-advocacy, you will be able to stand up not only for yourself but for what you believe a relationship should be: one that serves both of you equally and helps you both become more than either of you could ever be on your own.

— Stan Tatkin, PsyD, MFT
Calabasas, CA, March 2013

Acknowledgments

Many people contributed to this book. First, I want to thank all my patients—whether in a recovering relationship or not—for allowing me the privilege of witnessing your sorrows, joys, and transformations. Whether you realize it or not, as each of you generously share the intimacies of your life, you are giving profound meaning to mine. And, without you, this book would not have been possible.

I want to thank the many meditation teachers I have had over the course of my lifetime, especially Trudy Goodman and Christiane Wolf, my MBSR teachers. They brought meditation back into my life at a time when my spirit most needed it. They are also responsible for my love of mindfulness meditation and are the reason that it is the theoretical underpinning of this book. I am also indebted to the founders of Alcoholics Anonymous, Dr. Bob and Bill Wilson, as well as the founders of Al-Anon, Lois W. and Anne B. The 12 step programs lifted me out of a progressive decline into the depths of insanity and have kept me on a steady trajectory toward liberation, growth, and happiness since 1982.

I want to give thanks to Jude Berman, who with her extraordinary editorial skill fought relentlessly with me to preserve intelligence and humor in my writing. I will be forever grateful to my brilliant goddaughter, Alexa Margalith, who held my hand from the first word to the last.

Thank you to the editors at New Harbinger Publications—Jess Beebe, Angela Autry Gorden, Tesilya Hanauer, and Nicola Skidmore—and copyeditor Ken Knabb for their enormous help in shaping the book and bringing it to the finishing line.

Introduction

Few challenges in life are more difficult than being in a committed relationship with an addict. I say this having worked in the field of mental health and addiction recovery since 1982. During this time, I've come across hundreds of partners who, like you, loved someone who had an active addiction and continued to love that same person in his or her recovery.

From the moment your partner gets into recovery, you may feel confused about how to juggle being in a relationship with that person and staying free of old, enabling behaviors. You may find yourself struggling to keep your eyes off your partner and on yourself, while striving to build a strong connection—something you may have never had before.

Good news! It doesn't always have to be so hard. I've had the satisfaction of watching recovering couples overcome their challenges and move toward and into the quality of relationship they've always wanted and deserved. When I refer to a "couple in recovery," I mean a couple in which the addict gets clean and sober, and the partner recovers from obsessive caretaking, also known as *codependency*.

I live in Los Angeles, a land of new age psychology and therapy speak, where it's not uncommon to hear someone toss out the term "codependent" while sipping a chai latte. Though others may nod along as if they know exactly what it means, the truth is that the term is very often misunderstood and misused. So let me explain.

Codependency is an emotional and psychological state in which one is excessively preoccupied with taking care of or controlling another person at the expense of one's own needs. The key word here is "excessively." The codependent's excessive focus on caretaking does not only occur with his or her primary partner; it can also apply to work relationships, friendships, and relationships with extended family. People with codependency have a hard time leaving relationships that are abusive or depriving, tend to stay in jobs that are stressful, and are prone to ignoring their medical needs. Because of their high tolerance for denying their own needs, codependents tend to wait until they have experienced serious consequences before seeking a path of recovery.

Simply put, if you're a codependent, you have formed your identity around the need to be needed. You hope that if you put enough gas in the tank of others by taking care of them, they will be able to take care of you. Although you end up feeling empty or resentful, you continue to get involved with people you perceive you can rescue or fix. This makes you a magnet for addicts, and addicts a magnet for you.

If you are in a committed partnership with a recovering addict, I'm willing to bet you are or have been struggling with codependency. I have included many examples throughout this book that illustrate how codependents think, feel, and act before recovery, and how they think, feel, and act as recovering codependents. This book is meant to help you recover from codependency and remain with your recovering partner over the long haul—not like a POW held in captivity within a hostile relationship, but as a free agent happy to come home to your partner at the end of each and every day.

How This Book Came to Be

During the twenty years my husband, Brian, and I have been together, we've always had support from a vast network of loving friends and family. Even so, we needed the help of experts to ensure we stayed closer to love than to war. We tried a myriad of couple-improvement programs while "trudging the road of happy destiny" together by working the 12 steps and remaining actively involved with a community of those in recovery. These programs were, and remain, the foundation for our lives, emotionally and spiritually. We used them before we met and continued to do so after we became a committed couple.

Ultimately, this is the book I wish I'd been able to read when my husband and I first got married. Although some resources were available for the painful dynamics we kept bumping up against, I had so many questions hanging on the coatrack of shame that I needed a book like this to magically show up in my mailbox—nicely wrapped in brown paper, please! I mean, how do you ask bookstore salespeople if they have any good books for couples who come from family trees riddled with alcoholism and addiction, and who are kind of oppositional, defiant, and tyrannical themselves, yet who want to learn how to be slightly more cooperative and a lot less resentful?

In the tenth year of our marriage, my husband and I decided to take a mindfulness-based stress reduction (MBSR) course because we had heard it helped lessen reactivity and increased well-being. Jon Kabat-Zinn created MBSR in 1979 at the University of Massachusetts Medical Center in an effort to help medical patients learn a meditative practice known as mindfulness. Kabat-Zinn's mission was to help lower health costs and to bring about awareness of the benefits of a holistic approach to illness. The results were literally mind-boggling: research using fMRI (functional magnetic resonance imaging) indicated structural change in the brains of people who practiced mindfulness meditation. Harvard researchers Sara Lazar (2000) and Britta K. Hölzel (2010, 2011) and their colleagues studied brain scans of meditators who had received the MBSR training and found that the density of gray matter in their hippocampus (associated with learning) increased, while the density of gray matter in their amygdala (associated with stress and fear) decreased. When the researchers compared these brain scans with scans of individuals who had not received the training, they did not find the same changes. This strongly suggests that the brain can rewire emotional patterns so that individuals are better able to manage their emotional responses to stress.

MBSR offered a method for lowering the level of stress my husband and I had been living with at the time, which had negatively impacted the quality of our relationship. After the course, mindfulness meditation became part of our daily routine. The result was not only positive changes in how we went about our days individually, but dramatic changes in the atmosphere between us, as well.

My method draws on Kabat-Zinn's (1990) MBSR approach as well as on attachment theory, as defined by John Bowlby, Mary Ainsworth, and other psychologists. In essence, the style of parenting you experienced while growing up determines how easily you are able to create a secure and satisfying bond with a romantic partner as an adult. To heal as a codependent in recovery, you need to develop the ability to form a secure and lasting bond with your partner. MBSR provides some of the most powerful techniques I have seen to accomplish this, so I have incorporated them in my workshops and in this book. As you read this book, I will introduce you to the following ten skills:

1. How to start your day feeling calm and mindful

2. How to check in with yourself during the day and retrieve a sense of calm

3. How to sustain a separate sense of self and set appropriate boundaries, while remaining connected to your partner

4. How to handle strong emotions without becoming overwhelmed

5. How to get in touch with gratitude and overcome feelings of resentment

6. How to be present with your partner and allow love to flow from there

7. How to nourish intimacy in the present moment

8. How to communicate with your partner without becoming caught up in judgments or negative emotions

9. How to enhance the spiritual dimension of your relationship through mindfulness practice

10. How to use mindfulness to prevent emotional relapse

Unfortunately, for each couple I see succeed with these skills, there are countless others who will never have the benefit of qualified professional help in their healing. They're left on their own. In the hope of helping some of these couples, I decided to put my methods into book form. I began by documenting the most common questions my clients and workshop participants expressed to me, as well as the practical advice and answers I gave them. Then I assembled the mindfulness exercises and other techniques that my clients have found most helpful.

How to Use This Book

This book is highly practical and earnestly devoted to the actualization of your life. Each chapter features a variety of exercises, including at least one mindfulness meditation. Because your partner most likely will not be sitting next to you as you read this book, the majority of exercises can be done alone. I also offer solo options for the few exercises that are designed for couples to do together.

You can stop and do the exercises and meditations as you read, or come back and do them later in the day or week. Some of them may speak more directly to you than others, but I suggest you give them all at least one try. Then you can build a daily practice with the ones that resonate most for you. If a suggestion doesn't resonate with you at first, just try it one more time. If you don't notice any benefit after that, it probably isn't right for you.

The more you practice and experiment with these techniques, the easier you'll find them to be. Moreover, as you practice, the issues that make your relationship feel so hard should start to become easier.

Learning to be mindful in your thoughts, feelings, and actions will help you stay steady in the face of all that comes up in the context of your relationship—conflicts; daily stressors; illness; job loss; money problems; raising kids; and even the scariest thought of all, your partner having a relapse. At the same time, by learning to be mindful, you can put some savings in the bank to protect yourself from your own emotional relapse.

As you become more mindful, you can expect to:

- Feel love for yourself and for your partner.

- Be able to listen better to your partner.

- Establish trust, overcome betrayal, and find forgiveness.

- Feel appreciated and have gratitude for your partnership.

- Let go of self-criticalness.

- Know when to assert yourself and when to go with the flow.

- Be able to give your partner the benefit of the doubt, even when he or she is behaving insensitively.

- Maintain your sense of humor, even when the going gets rough.

- Feel greater self-acceptance and self-confidence, and less fear.

- Have "go-to" strategies for when boredom, fear, indifference, or murderous rage toward your partner rear their ugly heads.

- Know what to do if your partner relapses.

Ultimately, I wrote *Loving Someone in Recovery* to promote the values of kindness, compassion, and connection that are possible between partners in a committed relationship once addiction has been arrested and recovery has taken its place. Of course, there are never guarantees in life and love, but once you make the decision to become a change agent, and steer yourself away from unhealthy entanglement and into healthy connection (focus on taking better care of yourself while letting your recovering partner find how to live a sober life without you having to be his or her life coach) the likelihood of your relationship lasting immediately jumps. And, trust me, success can occur even if both of you are not waking up to recovery at the exact same time or the exact same speed.

Yes, it can be tough. But in my experience, most people can succeed if they're armed with the right skills. My goal is to give you mindful and effective tools to replace the ones that aren't so mindful or effective, so that slowly but surely you go from disconnection to connection, from unconsciousness to consciousness; from suffering to joy.

CHAPTER 1

Taking the Struggle out of Recovery

If you love someone in recovery and are seeking help—whether from a therapist, an addiction professional, a 12-step program, or some other spiritual path—keep in mind that any map you find will be just that. It is not a guarantee of success or a foolproof solution. That includes this book. You can look at this book as a road map to help you see your relationship in a new way. Regardless of how distant or alienated you may be feeling from your partner right now, it can help you inch your way closer to your partner mentally, emotionally, physically, and spiritually.

The main tool I offer in this book, mindfulness, could be said to work a lot like a global positioning system. The wonder of a GPS is that it always knows exactly where you are. It doesn't provide a lot of useless information (at least when it's working properly); it just says, "Here is where you are." When you move, it knows exactly where you are in that next moment, too. In this way, moment by moment, it gets you to where you want to go. Having this ready guidance can save you a lot of angst and worry about whether you will reach your destination.

Think of mindfulness as your internal GPS. As you move away from self-defeating behaviors that you habitually engage in with your recovering partner, mindfulness will track your efforts to stay the course toward your destination of new and more fulfilling behaviors.

Just Add Mindfulness

Mindfulness meditation has been practiced in Asia for thousands of years. During the last several decades, Western psychologists have begun to use it as a therapeutic technique, and with great success, as Daphne Davis and Jeffrey Hayes from Pennsylvania State University report (2011). Research has shown the benefits of mindfulness meditation for general well-being as well as for helping get one's reactivity under control before it can disrupt the connection with one's partner. The careful and attentive practice of mindfulness meditation can help you cope with, rather than just survive, the constant flow of change that occurs in life. Mindfulness is a state that only requires you to be observational of your ever-changing moods, emotions, sensations, and thoughts.

You may not immediately imagine the benefits of sitting quietly next to your partner for a mere two minutes a day, but there are plenty. Your relationship experiences many twists and turns on a daily basis, and mindfulness will strengthen your nervous system to counterbalance the huge negatives of stress and overreactivity and allow you to be creative and hearty in your responses to your recovering partner. In addition, mindfulness has been used to treat stress, anxiety, depression, and substance abuse, among other things, and has been shown to help prevent relapse among recovering addicts.

I have been practicing mindfulness personally on a daily basis and folding it into my clients' therapy, as well. Simply put, mindfulness is what it sounds like it is—being mindful. Whether you do it alone or with your partner, mindfulness meditation is simply the act of paying attention to your breath without trying to control it, and observing thoughts, feelings, and sensations. If you can bring this level of awareness to each and every waking moment, you are living mindfully.

In this book you will learn three essential practices of mindfulness:

1. Being aware

2. Being present

3. Being nonjudgmental

Let's look briefly at the power of each of these practices.

Be Aware: You Are the Observer of Your World

Normally we live life amid a vast flux of thought and emotions. Our partner says something and we react automatically. Mindfulness adds the practice of being aware, or being the observer, of all that is happening. In and of itself, this does not appear to have much effect, yet it has a big impact when you aim to heal your relationship with a partner in recovery. For example, if you snap at your partner when he or she says something you disapprove of, observing the sensations in your body and any images, smells, sights, or memories that come up can give you insight into why your first response was to snap. When you are aware and observant, you are open to learning and to the possibility of new feelings and fresh ways of responding.

Be Present: The Key to Change Rests in the Present Moment

Much of the time, our minds are consumed by thoughts of the past or the future. We fret and obsess over what has already happened, and we worry about what has not happened yet. Mindfulness teaches the axiom that those on a 12-step path already live by: Take one day at a time. When you love someone in recovery, the best way to transform your relationship is to perpetually approach it from the perspective of the present moment.

Be Nonjudgmental: True Loving Is Based on Acceptance of Yourself and Others

When you practice being an aware observer in each moment, you create a new basis for loving your partner. You can stop being critical or negative or judgmental—both of your partner and of yourself. Instead, mindfulness teaches the value of acceptance and unconditional positive regard. You may not like what your partner says or does, or does not say or do, but you can practice acceptance of your relationship as it is.

Breaking the habit of being self-critical or critical of your partner takes time; that is why it is called a "practice" and not a "done deal." First you must become aware of exactly when your mind is generating a critical voice. Then you can look for what is behind the criticalness. Usually a critical mind is the result of feeling disappointed, hurt, or afraid. Recognizing and connecting with who you are beneath your critical mind—the person who is in pain—allows you to start being more compassionate toward yourself, instead of getting lost in judgment.

In the chapters that follow, we will look at how to put each of these practices to use in your life and your relationship.

MINDFULNESS MEDITATION:
Watching, Watching, Watching

The most basic form of mindfulness meditation is very simple. It involves watching the most essential natural process of your existence: your breath.

Read these instructions to yourself, then put down the book and do the meditation.

1. Take a moment to sit back in your chair and get comfortable.

2. Close your eyes.

3. Take a deep breath in and a long, slow breath out, and allow yourself to relax.

4. Let your breathing resume its normal rate. Don't force it to change in any way. Just observe it.

5. "Watch" your breath as it flows in and out. Don't do anything else. Just watch.

6. Thoughts may come to mind and distract you from observing your breath. As soon as you become aware of this happening, turn your attention back to watching your breath.

7. When you are ready, open your eyes.

You can do this mindfulness meditation every morning as a means to start the day in a calm manner. You can also do it in the evening to end the day, as well as at any point along the way when you check in with yourself and sense the need to calm down. You don't have to spend a long time at it, either. Experiment and see how many minutes of watching, watching, watching you need to feel the effects. Sometimes it may be enough just to whisper "Watching, watching, watching!" to yourself. The more you practice mindfulness, the less time it will take. Of course, you may choose to enjoy the space of mindful meditation for as long as you wish.

The Struggle Spectrum

What I especially appreciate about the mindfulness practices of being aware, being present, and being nonjudgmental is their ability to take the struggle out of loving someone in recovery.

Here is a list of statements codependent people who love someone in recovery typically make about themselves when asked about the cause of their struggles. Do you identify with any of these?

- I cannot let others take care of me.

- I am extremely loyal, and I put up with situations for far too long.

- I cannot help thinking that I know better how the people I love should be living their lives than they do.

- I have to be needed in my relationship to feel secure.

- I do not like feeling vulnerable with my partner.

- I ignore my partner's unavailability, and instead put hope in an imaginary future.

- I feel anxious when my partner tries to compliment me, give me gifts, or offer praise.

- It is nearly impossible for me to admit to my partner when I've made a mistake.

- I hide the difficulties I am having in my relationship because I feel ashamed.

- I am self-critical and can be harshly critical of my partner, as well.

- I am highly resistant to being in recovery and do not like to be told what to do.

- I pull my partner toward me, but when he or she gets close, I push him or her away.

- I run from my suffering and mask my pain with humor, deflection, or isolation.

- It is nearly impossible to face my true feelings in front of my partner without becoming anxious.

When we look closely at these causes of struggle, it's clear that maintaining a committed, long-term relationship with a partner in recovery can be really tough at times. Having worked with hundreds of couples, both with and without addiction, I know that a committed partnership is not easy for anyone to maintain. It does take some daily concentrated effort to recover from codependency. But you can do it. By allowing yourself to seek advice and education, you're already moving in a positive direction!

Those who love someone in recovery face a wide range of struggles. On one end of the spectrum, emotions can be explosive and the relationship can feel suffocating. On the other end, one or both partners can become so disconnected they feel as though they are not in a relationship at all. Suffice it to say, every couple in recovery is a work in progress. You can take comfort from the fact that there isn't a person on this earth who loves someone in recovery who is not wrestling with some of the same issues you already have or are going to have during the lifespan of your relationship.

Even if you were to say that today you are at 10 on a scale of 1 to 10 (where 10 is all-out war in your relationship), there is still room to move to 9. Let's at least say that, for now, if your partner has kicked his or her addiction, that battle is over and the road to recovery has taken its place.

As long as there is still a stone left unturned by you, there is hope for making your relationship a better one. You may not yet know what that stone might be, but perhaps you will learn as you keep reading.

So please don't be discouraged if your relationship is starting out in the red. Today really is a new day, and change is possible!

The Codependent and the Addict

This book is for anyone in a committed relationship whose partner has chosen to embark on a path of recovery from addiction. When I use the term *recovery*, I am referring to the process of abstaining from addiction while also living a robust life of love and service with friends and family and sustaining a spiritual practice and hearty involvement with the community at large. I use this definition, based on one developed by the Betty Ford Institute (2007), because it clarifies that recovery is more than mere sobriety.

When I use the term *addiction*, I am referring to all types of addictions. This book was written for you if any of the following addictions are, or have been, part of your partner's life:

- Drugs

- Alcohol

- Gambling

- Sex

- Exercise

- Work

- Technology (Internet, Facebook)

- Religion

- Pornography

- Shopping

- Food

- Video games

- Anything else the craving brain can use and abuse

In other words, I'm not just talking about the obvious addictions that cause significant physical dependency, such as drugs and alcohol. I'm also talking about process addictions, which do not necessarily cause physical dependency but can become psychologically all-consuming. A process addiction is any repeated behavior, not involving the ingestion of addictive substances, that a person does not stop, despite loss of enjoyment and impaired thinking, and that gets progressively worse over time, never better.

I should add that although we say an addict or alcoholic has a disease, we don't say that a codependent has the disease of codependency. We don't blame codependency on genetics, either. Rather, codependency is almost always a result of growing up in a family system in which the child is called upon, covertly or overtly, to care for people long before that would be developmentally appropriate. For example, a child whose parent is an alcoholic may sense from an early age that Mom or Dad needs caretaking and can't handle the normal demands of parenting. As a result, codependent pathways are carved out in the brain. Instead of cultivating the ability to bond with others, the child's brain focuses on becoming masterful at sensing others' needs.

Some people do define codependency as a process addiction, however. But what distinguishes codependency from other process addictions is that codependents are addicted to the people they love, and they end up relating to them in ways they cannot stop, regardless of the negative impact on their health and emotional well-being.

Why Do You Love Each Other?

Let me be straight about why the codependent and the addict fit perfectly together. They fit because they will stay together through thick and thin, even going so far as to stick together until addiction practically kills them both. It can be difficult to understand how the codependent has as much work to do on himself or herself as the recovering addict has. The thinking of the partner of the addict may be innocently misguided, but it is just as mixed up as that of the addict. The relationship you have together is a *folie à deux*, or "a craziness of two." It is a craziness you both have, and it is a craziness from which you need to recover as much as your addict partner does.

When I say craziness, I'm not referring to certifiable. I mean the kind of distorted thinking that results when you mix addiction, codependency, and relationships together. Fortunately, as a codependent, you can get well and actualize yourself, just as an addict can recover from any other form of addiction.

For starters, ask yourself several quick questions:

- Am I good at finishing my partner's sentences?

- Do I help my partner in ways that others I love and respect tell me are against my own best interests?

- Do I feel responsible for my partner's every move?

- Am I only truly comfortable when my partner is in close proximity to me?

If you answered yes to any of these questions, welcome to the codependency club!

Don't get me wrong—just because you struggle with codependency doesn't mean you're a bad person or are suffering from a terminal diagnosis. The truth is, you're just very anxious and prone to worry, and you assuage your anxiety by hyperfocusing on your partner's problems. You're willing to invest your life in someone who is an active addict—rather than being with someone who doesn't need to be saved by you—because you have a knack for seeing potential in everyone, even if that potential is nowhere to be seen by the person himself or herself! You can spend an enormous amount of time trying to help your partner reach his or her potential, even when your partner hasn't asked this of you.

Here are some of the typical misguided ideas with which codependents struggle:

- You equate being totally responsible for your partner with love.

- You do for your partner what he or she needs to do for himself or herself.

- You let others have their way, and then you feel hurt and resentful.

- You work hard not to have needs, seeing this as a measuring stick for your own goodness.

- You continually talk, worry, or think about your partner and his or her problems.

- You get overly involved in your partner's business.

- You pick partners who are unavailable or too wounded to be able to care for you.

- You think that controlling your partner, who is either an active addict or a recovering addict, is the way to get your needs met.

Unlike drug addicts or alcoholics, codependents will not become progressively less functional and suffer consequences such as lost jobs, poor health, and conflict with family and friends. You aren't going to get fired from your job for being nice, being punctual, remembering every staff member's birthday, or striving compulsively for perfection.

You won't lose friends from being highly reliable and filled with sympathy for those less fortunate. No one ever complains about having to pick a codependent off the floor and clean up his or her mess. This is why it can take so much longer for you as a codependent to face your own issues and take those issues as seriously as you take your partner's.

There is a huge difference between a caring person and a codependent one. The caring person without codependency issues won't stay long in a relationship with anyone who is unavailable, wounded, or an addict and is not helping himself or herself get well. Rather than run, a codependent will try to pick up the pieces and feel drawn even closer to the person he or she loves. As the addict gets worse, the codependent's helping behavior becomes more and more consuming and compulsive.

Are You a Double Winner?

You may be wondering if one can be an addict and a codependent at the same time. The answer is yes. The term used in the recovery community to describe people with both addiction and codependency issues is *double winner*.

For example, Sara is in recovery from alcoholism. As she gets some clean and sober time under her belt, she begins dealing with issues beyond physical sobriety. At this point, codependent tendencies begin to surface. Instead of focusing on her own program, she finds herself obsessively concerned with the minutiae in the everyday life of her partner, Chris. Hence, Sara is a double winner.

The same can occur in reverse. Chris is codependently involved with Sara. When she gets sober, instead of embracing his own autonomy, Chris begins to fill the void by becoming a workaholic. Boom! Now Chris is also a double winner because he is suffering from both codependency and addiction.

Just as addicts can learn to live an addiction-free life, codependents can recover from the obsessive need to control and be emotionally overinvolved with the partners they love to the detriment of themselves. And double winners can do the same.

To Seek Therapy or Not to Seek Therapy

As I've said, you don't have to be in therapy to read this book. Nonetheless, therapy may be on your mind. Perhaps you are avoiding therapy because you fear there is something inherently, horribly wrong with you and don't want that exposed. You don't want to risk a therapist confirming your worst fears. If you feel you need more support than you are getting, you shouldn't allow fear or self-judgment to stop you. A good therapist will emphasize your strengths over your weaknesses and offer ways to foster self-love, not more self-criticalness.

Regardless of whether you seek therapy, either with your partner or alone, stay focused on what you are doing right. In other words, it's time to stop judging yourself for all the things you think you did wrong in the relationship. Life can be really hard, and you may think your situation will always be the same. In fact, this mind-set is counterproductive. In this book, and as a therapist, I encourage you to empower yourself. And I don't mean this in some cotton-candy way. I'm fully aware there are people out there who've done some really hurtful things to their partners. You may even be one of them. It just doesn't help to highlight your past bad behavior with shame and self-rejection when you are trying to become a better person.

First Steps on Your Path of Recovery

Your recovery as a codependent begins when you start to develop boundaries around your compulsive need to take care of others. I will address the subject of boundaries in much more detail in chapter 3. For now, you can start developing and understanding what your boundaries are by taking notice of both your positive and your negative reactions to others. These reactions dictate your boundaries, and help you consider what course of actions to take. Let's break it out into some first steps that you can do right now.

TRY THIS: Brave It

Set a positive intention for yourself. For starters, repeat the following series of statements to yourself:

- "I am going to brave knowing myself."

- "I'm going to brave being in touch with my feelings and not distracting myself by focusing on my partner."

- "I'm going to start being mindful of the impulse to help my recovering partner."

- "Instead of jumping to help my partner, I'm going to sit still and breathe until the impulse calms down."

Can you say this? Even silently to yourself, in the privacy of your own mind? I'm not expecting you to live up to each statement 100 percent the first time you say it. But know that just the act of making positive statements like this, called *affirmations*, to yourself can have a powerful effect. Saying "I'm going to brave..." sets you up to feel braver. When you think of it this way, it's not so hard, right? In fact, if you can say it even once, you're on the road of your own recovery program.

MINDFULNESS MEDITATION:
Mindfully Get Back to Your Self

In any given moment, you have the power to stop and check in with yourself. This exercise will guide you through the simplest, most basic practice of mindfulness. Right now, take five minutes to check in and observe yourself in a mindful way.

Make sure you are sitting comfortably, somewhere no one is going to disturb you for these few minutes.

1. Notice how it feels to be in your body. Scan each part of your body and notice the sensations you feel. What sensations are you experiencing in your head? Is it warm? Does it feel tingly? Or heavy? Any tight muscles? What about your neck? Your shoulders? Your hands? Can you feel your heart beat? What sensations do you feel in your stomach? Your knees? Your big toe? Don't try to change anything. Just observe. That's being mindful.

2. Also be aware of your breathing. Are you holding your breath? Is your breathing shallow or deep?

3. Check in with yourself at the emotional level. The sensations associated with emotions may seem subtler than the sensations you feel at the purely physical level. Are you feeling mad, sad, glad, or afraid? Nothing at all? Whatever it is, again, don't try to change it. Allow yourself to have whatever feelings arise.

4. Check in with your mind. Undoubtedly you are thinking about something, even if only this exercise and the emotions you just observed. Your mind is always with you, and it always has something to say, doesn't it?

    For just this moment, see if you can let your mind take a rest from attempting to fix anything or anybody. Let it roll

23

on by. Don't try to stop it, control it, or resist it. Instead, let your thoughts be there, but put your attention back onto the sensations in your body. Stop giving your thoughts the usual attention and take note of the sensations and feelings going on within you.

5. With each breath you take, allow yourself to relax more deeply. Drop your shoulders and release any tension in your belly. Be curious, rather than judgmental. As a mindful meditator, you are now witnessing your experience, taking it all in. Notice that when you allow your thoughts and feelings to be as they are, they seem to float on by, and you don't get stuck or bogged down with them.

6. For the rest of the day, make an effort to be especially mindful of your thoughts, sensations, and emotions, while remaining present in your surroundings.

Notice how you feel after you have done this mindfulness meditation.

The Relationship Quiz

In the chapters that follow, I'm going to share with you things that people who love partners in recovery have done, alone and with their partner, to successfully create new avenues in their relationships. In other words, help is on the way! However, before you begin to make changes in your relationship, you need to know where you stand and what you believe in general about what makes a loving partnership sustainable over the long term.

I like to use this quiz with couples the first time I meet them. I tell them it's like putting a head on top of your head, in the sense that it's a way to witness your own mind. Once you know what is in your mind, it is easier to decide whether you want to go along with and act out what your thoughts are telling you to do. One interesting thing about mindfulness is that it teaches you not to resist what you are thinking, yet it gives you the power to know clearly what you are thinking. Hopefully you began to experience this as you did the "Mindfully Get Back to Your Self" exercise.

Before you read further in this book, take three minutes to complete this quiz. Write your answers to each question (either true or false) on a piece of paper. That way you can take the quiz again after you have read the book and worked through the techniques in it, and see if any of your answers have changed.

1. If my recovering partner and I just talk enough about our problems, they will be solved.

   TRUE   FALSE

2. If my recovering partner and I just stop talking about our problems, they will be solved.

   TRUE   FALSE

3. Our relationship will take care of itself; my job is to just take care of myself.

   TRUE   FALSE

4. My recovering partner and I must always be working together on our relationship at the same time for it to succeed.

   TRUE   FALSE

5. Even with the right support, my recovering partner and I will never be able to trust each other completely.

   TRUE   FALSE

6. Not having any sex with my recovering partner is better for our relationship than having mediocre sex.

   TRUE   FALSE

7. Sexual desire has gone away for my recovering partner and me over time, but that's normal in a long-term partnership.

   TRUE   FALSE

8. Resolving all the differences between my recovering partner and me is the key to our long-term, sustainable, and fulfilling future together.

   TRUE   FALSE

9. Having expectations of my recovering partner helps him or her grow.

   TRUE   FALSE

10. The growth of our relationship is dependent on my recovering partner making certain changes in himself or herself.

    TRUE   FALSE

11. The growth of our relationship is dependent on my making certain changes in myself.

    TRUE   FALSE

12. As long as we stay together, time will heal our wounds.

    TRUE   FALSE

After you have finished, you may want to share the quiz with your partner. If you ask nicely, he or she may be willing to take it, too, though that isn't essential.

Keep in mind that there are no wrong answers. This quiz is merely about what you believe to be true. However, some of what you currently believe, especially as you take this quiz for the first time, may no longer be effective in creating the kind of relationship you want to have. So, as you review your answers, consider what they might mean for your relationship. For example, if you answered "True" to the statement "If my recovering partner and I just talk enough about our problems, they will be solved," what does that mean for how you speak to your partner—how often, and about what? Each answer you give may inspire further thought about how you view intimate relationships and how you can build the kind of relationship you truly want.

The road to your recovery from codependency cannot be built overnight. But little by little, as you think about your answers to the Relationship Quiz, learn from my answers to the common questions that partners of a recovering addict have, and do the exercises throughout the book, you may just end up existing happily within your relationship in a way that you never thought possible.

CHAPTER 2

Getting Acquainted with Addiction-Free Reality: Breaking the Fantasy Spells

Now that recovery has entered your home, you can use it to get off the merry-go-round of black-and-white, overly simplistic thinking characteristic of addiction and codependency. Become acquainted instead with reality as perceived by the gray matter of a balanced mind. As you've surely noticed, you and your partner are complex people. We might say that the wheel that makes each of you who you are has many spokes. This chapter will delve into these spokes, with respect to your stage of recovery, frame of reference for your relationship, value system, and self-acceptance. These spokes take time to get to know, and a lifetime to fully understand. So stand up and get ready to meet yourself and your partner, for real this time. Welcome to recovery.

You may feel as though your relationship has been given a stay of execution after your partner enters recovery. The fantasy that your relationship will be miraculously restored and your longing for emotional nourishment met may fill you with an enormous sense of expectation. Finally, you're now both there to support each other, and it is your turn to have your life witnessed by a clear-headed, loving partner. After all, this is your new, addiction-free reality!

Unfortunately, recovery isn't always such a simple transition. In fact, partners who love someone at the starting gate of recovery can find themselves feeling they have nothing in common with their partner, beyond wanting addiction out of their lives for good. Recovery can be so consuming that it is hard to see what else you have in common. If something like this happens to you, hold your horses. The truth is, you don't really know what potential your relationship holds. And this is not the time to make snap judgments. Nor is it the time to build castles in the sky. You've been hurt by unfulfilled expectations and fantasies for far too long already.

Now is your chance to find out how you can break this spell and keep both feet on the ground. I can't say this enough: The slower you go, the faster you will get where you are trying to get with your partner. That might sound counterintuitive, but it is true. Impatience and frustration and taking shortcuts are the old means of addictive living. Give yourself time to think, sort things out, and get things right.

Many people in a relationship with a recovering addict wonder, "Just how much unhappiness and frustration am I supposed to put up with? How do I know when I should call it quits?"

Only you can answer these questions. I've seen couples who appear to be doing fine together end up in an acrimonious divorce. On the other hand, some couples who fight constantly stay together for many, many years. Their deal breakers come and go, yet they continue walking hand in hand. So don't let anyone tell you when it's time to give up on the struggle to work things out. You may get help from outside resources or consultants, but ultimately, the decision is yours.

Refrain from making judgments at this point, however, about whether you are going to stay together or split. Instead, indulge yourself by spending time making things better for yourself and see if that improves the relationship.

Stages of Recovery

Recovery can be divided into two stages: first stage recovery and second stage recovery. The notion of stages originated in the world of substance abuse treatment, but it is equally applicable to all types of addiction. These stages include the recovery process of the codependent. Getting familiar with the characteristics of these stages is helpful because you and your relationship are functioning in one of them. Generally, people assume that the stage they are in depends on the amount of time they've been in recovery. This is not true. The stage of recovery you are in is determined not by time, but by the way you both behave, the attitudes you hold, and how much introspective work you have done. Among other things, this chapter will help you understand what the different stages of recovery look like and what you might expect to experience in each.

First Stage Recovery

You may have woken up one morning and decided you were done revolving around your partner's addiction and were ready to get help. You may have prayed for a long time to get the courage to take this step, and then a window of opportunity opened up and you took it. Or maybe your addicted partner hurt you one too many times, and that was the final straw. Whichever way, when you made the decision to stop being overly concerned with your partner and start focusing on your own well-being instead, you entered first stage recovery.

Sometimes addicts are punted into first stage recovery by an accident, a family intervention, the threat of divorce, being fired from a job, a mental breakdown, or a physical illness. In any case, no one skips merrily into first stage recovery. You'll never hear someone say, "When I was a child, I fantasized about growing up and getting caught up in addiction, ruining everything I was striving for, and then having to spend time each day learning how to live comfortably in my own skin while abstaining from my addiction." Or on your end, "When I was a child, I fantasized about finding an addict partner whom I could be consumed with taking care of, and then having to spend time each day recovering from codependency."

First stage recovery exists for both the addict and the codependent. It's important to know that your partner's decision to get clean and sober and step into first stage recovery doesn't automatically put you into first stage recovery, as well. Your first stage recovery comes when you have your own awakening and realize that you are done trying to rescue your partner and are ready to face yourself instead.

You may have wanted to leave your partner while addiction was in the picture. But you couldn't. And you didn't, at least not permanently. That isn't because you were naïve or weak. It is because you became attached to your partner and desperately hoped your love would conquer all. You were convinced it was only a matter of time and a few nudges before your dear one stopped drinking, taking drugs, overspending, under- or overeating, texting obsessively— stopped doing whatever was consuming his or her life. Even in the face of addiction, you always felt a small pulse of hope flowing through your veins. As Cicero once said, "While there's life, there's hope."

Although no longer active in their addictions, both the addict and the codependent in first stage recovery are still struggling with getting the outside support they need, and grappling with mixed feelings and fears about what it means to be completely clean of addiction and codependency. For example, most addicts entering first stage recovery are still hoping their excessive use was simply a function of things getting a little out of control due to a heavy dose of life stressors or underlying issues. They may be scared to seriously consider and call their behavior an addiction. They may be even more resistant to the idea that they have a "disease" that is driven by their genetic makeup or a condition determined by neurotransmitters in their brain. There is ample denial in this stage. Typically, addicts go back and forth on whether or not to make being in recovery a lifelong choice.

Codependents are equally baffled at this stage. You may still think the blame for your obsessive efforts to control your partner falls entirely on his or her addiction. You may find yourself still bargaining with your partner or trying to hold his or her feet to the fire, so that he or she is forced to let go of that addiction once and for all. You still aren't sure that your level of involvement with your partner is really problematic. What you desperately need is a clearer picture of what it looks like to move from being an active codependent to being one in the first stage of recovery from codependency.

TRY THIS: What Stage Are You In?

It's a good idea to take stock of which stage of recovery you are currently in. Be as honest as you can with yourself so that you can get to know yourself better. Don't take this as one more reason to get down on yourself. There are no wrong answers in this exercise. I mean it: *there are no wrong answers in this exercise*. The most important thing is simply being honest with yourself. Mindfully go over each statement. Remember to breathe, and notice what comes up within you as you do.

Respond to each of the following statements with a yes ("this describes me") or no ("this does not describe me"):

_____ I feel bored and lonely if my recovering partner goes out with his or her friends at night.

_____ I feel anxious if I go out with my friends and I'm gone too long.

_____ I feel left out if my recovering partner doesn't tell me the details of what he or she does when not with me.

_____ I always need to know what my recovering partner is thinking about.

_____ It is hard for me to consider doing something I like without making sure my recovering partner approves of it.

_____ I find it hard to stay friends with people my recovering partner doesn't like.

_____ I find it hard to accept that my recovering partner stays friends with people I don't like.

_____ I would feel hurt if my recovering partner wanted to go on a vacation with his or her friends and not with me.

_____ I don't understand why my recovering partner needs alone time when we could be together having fun.

_____ I hate that my recovering partner was close to anyone else romantically before being with me.

_____ I think it is important to read the same books.

_____ I don't like how much time my recovering partner spends talking on the phone with friends or family.

_____ I don't like the friends my recovering partner has on Facebook.

_____ I text my partner once an hour during my workday.

_____ I have difficulty identifying what I am feeling.

_____ I minimize, alter, or deny how I truly feel.

_____ I perceive myself as unselfish and dedicated to the well-being of others.

_____ I believe my recovering partner has trouble taking care of himself or herself.

_____ I try to convince my recovering partner of what to think, do, or feel.

_____ I freely offer my recovering partner advice and direction without being asked, but I become resentful when he or she declines my help or rejects my advice.

_____ I lavish gifts and favors on my recovering partner, even when we are not getting along.

_____ I use sexual attention to gain approval and acceptance from my recovering partner.

_____ I have to be needed by my recovering partner most of the time.

_____ I use blame and guilt to control my recovering partner.

Now count up the number of times you responded yes.

If you responded no to all the statements, you're beyond first stage recovery. You are in second stage recovery.

If you admitted to yourself that one to six statements describe you, it's time for you to practice greater independence from your partner because you are still struggling with issues of first stage recovery. After you do this, you should be able to move into second stage recovery with relative ease.

If you said seven to fifteen statements describe you, it is time for you to force yourself to find ways to enjoy alone time, get a hobby, or hang out with friends. For you, second stage recovery is probably still some ways around the bend.

If you said sixteen or more statements describe you, chances are you are barely hanging on to first stage recovery. If you aren't already going, it is time for you to seriously consider visiting an Al-Anon meeting.

Originally, Al-Anon was designed as a mutual-support group using the same 12 steps as Alcoholics Anonymous (AA), but for people experiencing a problem with someone else's drinking. Today, anyone is entitled to go to Al-Anon for a problem with someone else's addiction of any type. Al-Anon has no leaders, only volunteers, and just as with AA, you can find a meeting almost anywhere in the world, even online. Go to six meetings before you make a final decision about whether it is the support you need. The price is also right: you only have to put a dollar in the basket because there are no dues or fees. First-time visitors aren't even expected to put in a penny.

There is no need to white-knuckle your way alone through the process of abstaining from codependent habits. As you continue throwing yourself into the exercises in this book, and perhaps adding a little more outside help, you'll be moving steadily toward second stage recovery and transforming your life. So take a deep breath and dig in. Before you know it, you'll be a card-carrying member of the second stage recovery community!

Second Stage Recovery

As a codependent in second stage recovery, you take full responsibility for creating happiness in your life, as well as for doing what it takes to create harmony and connection with your beloved recovering partner. Second stage recovery is the point where you and your partner consciously start addressing matters beyond simply ceasing codependent or addictive behavior, including setting emotional boundaries, taking better care of your physical health, getting control over your own reactivity, and bringing intellectual clarity to the value system you want to live by. You are now willing to say, "My partner is recovering from the disease of addiction, and I am recovering from codependency." Naming your partner's addiction "a disease" liberates both of you from shame, self-blame, self-hatred, and self-incrimination.

Naming your own obsessive behavior, thoughts, and feelings as codependency will do the same. This is not a problem of morality, because you are not bad people trying to become good. Your partner is truly a victim of a disease, and both of you are trying to get well from the havoc that disease has wreaked on your lives.

I think the disease model makes a lot of sense. In fact, a growing body of research (Blum et al., 1990 and Montag, Kirsch, Sauer, Markett, and Reuter, 2012, among others) provides convincing evidence of genetic predisposition. This isn't to say that scientists expect to find a gene for every addiction. Rather, the idea is that some individuals possess a genetic makeup that predisposes them to get hooked to something. I won't bore you with details, but if you're curious, you can find mountains of research studies online by searching a few key words, such as "genetic loading," "addiction," and "alcoholism." I will tell you that the majority of people in recovery with whom I've worked can go on for days with stories about their relatives, near and far, who have struggled with all kinds of addiction.

You and your partner officially enter second stage recovery when your partner has taken addictive living off the table as an option, and you have done the same for codependent living; and when both of you have committed to an emotionally sober way of life. What this means is that you are committed to a way of life that is oriented toward greater awareness and collaborative effort, as we will be discussing throughout this book. In a nutshell, here are the attitudes and behaviors you can expect to own as a codependent in second stage recovery:

1. I'm willing to let my recovering partner serve my needs, even if it is done clumsily and imperfectly.

2. I know how to receive the love my recovering partner expresses for me.

3. I am willing to hear my recovering partner's apology when insult or injury has been inflicted.

4. I know how to show my recovering partner how to take care of me.

5. I make time to convey love to my recovering partner in ways I know he or she will appreciate.

6. I don't resent the burden of being in a committed relationship with a recovering addict.

7. I don't allow my recovering partner to take me for granted.

8. I am working toward expressing my erotic nature with my recovering partner.

9. I don't feel guilt or shame when my recovering partner shows sympathy or empathy for my suffering.

10. I mindfully exhale and let go of jealousy, hatred, indifference, and other negative feelings toward my recovering partner.

11. I practice mindfulness and feel moment-to-moment gratitude for my life and for my recovering partner, day or night.

12. I am grateful to have a path of recovery from codependency.

Second stage recovery demands that you transform yourself over time by unearthing unresolved emotional pain from your childhood that led you to become codependent and that you have yet to lay to rest. Second stage recovery can be a time of great introspection, during which you discover your identity both as an individual and as a partner.

As a codependent in second stage recovery, you will find yourself making the decision to let go of trying to change or control your partner—or, for that matter, trying to control the world around you. Instead, you will find greater connection to your vulnerability and risk exposing your needs to your partner. You will start to recoil naturally and quickly from operating out of stubborn willfulness and know whom to run to for help whenever you've impulsively tried to take control of your partner again.

The desire to avoid acting out of ego-driven, fear-based impulses becomes king at this phase of your recovery. You will have little to no interest in going back to the old, familiar, unconscious, controlling way of life you previously lived. Don't get me wrong, it's not that I think all our ego and efforts to control are the work of the devil. Everyone has an ego, and everyone is capable of muscling his or her way through the day. It's just that some people have a brand of ego that can land them in agitated, lonely, bitter, scary, or volatile places. Second stage recovery is about calming down that ego and being willing to wave a white flag.

If you find yourself in a constant power struggle with your partner and feel as if you are always going for a fight to the finish, then your ego is still in the driver's seat of the relationship. For you to succeed in recovery, your ego will need to back off a bit. By using mindfulness to get out of your ego and into your heart, you can take a more collaborative approach with your partner.

Moving from First Stage Recovery to Second Stage Recovery as a Couple

As you transition into second stage recovery, your days of living like two oxen on one yoke are over, and your days of clarifying your boundaries have begun. However, the movement from first stage recovery to second stage recovery is not something that happens quickly. In fact, you can stay stuck in first stage recovery long after your partner puts down his or her addiction and you renounce your codependency. Believing you can escape the normal suffering that comes with being in a committed relationship is wishful thinking that can keep you in the first stage. Think Peter Pan. Hoping to be rescued by someone who will fix the problems you face in your relationship is another way of thinking that will keep you stuck in first stage recovery. Again, think Peter Pan. Frankly, I've never met an addict in first stage recovery who didn't wish someone—that would be *you*, the codependent—would take over and do the work of living for him or her! That expectation is the essence of being in first stage recovery. Likewise, every codependent in first stage recovery would give their right arm for it to be their partner's fault that they act the way they do, and wishes that the changes their recovering partner makes would fix both of them!

Unfortunately, though, you can't have things both ways. You can't expect to have the benefits, rewards, and bonuses of second stage recovery while you continue to think and act like someone hanging back in first stage recovery. But you know what? You and your partner may have some sticky or complicated feelings to work through before second stage recovery makes sense to you. Therefore, you are free to stay in first stage recovery for as long as you need. Besides, you can never really be anywhere other than where you are. So just be mindfully aware of that, with no judgment or resistance.

The transition from first stage recovery to second stage recovery lies on a continuum—a line that runs from just entering the first stage to being fully established in the second stage. However, progress along the continuum is not necessarily linear. By this, I mean that you can be in second stage recovery one day and fall back into first stage recovery another. Or you can be in second stage recovery and your partner can be in first stage. Or vice versa. The reality is that people moving into second stage recovery do get off track and relapse. Your partner may pick up his or her addiction again, and you may start to get controlling in a way you thought you never again would. What can I say? Life can be a very messy and imperfect experience.

Now that you have a better idea about your own place on the continuum, let's meet some people in early second stage recovery. We begin with one of the most common questions that dazed and confused couples face after dipping their toes into the waters of second stage recovery.

Question: "Now That My Partner Is in Recovery, Why Hasn't Everything Fallen into Place Like I Imagined It Would?"

Kim and Jason were in their late twenties when they first met, and each was drawn to how charismatic, funny, and "hot" the other seemed. Both had done plenty of dating, and each told their respective friends that they were sure they'd found their soul mate within days of meeting each other. They described the honeymoon phase of their relationship as "a total blast." To quote Kim: "We were young and free from too much responsibility, and we could party like rock stars and still get up in the morning and go to work. I always knew Jason had the stamina to party harder than I could. What did I know? Everyone we knew was a self-proclaimed addict or alcoholic. Jason was actually proud of the amount of consumption he could handle and still be left standing. I know it sounds stupid now, but I was always very pleased with how well I could take care of everyone and make sure that no crisis happened. No one was going to drive home drunk on my watch, and I loved being the designated room mother for all my pals. Even if I had had any premonition about what we were going to go through for the last ten years, I probably still wouldn't have left."

Ten years and two young children—ages four and seven—later, they were dealing with Jason's second DUI in sixteen months. This time he was with his best friend, Mark, driving home from a party, when he hit a parked car. The impact threw Mark against the window and caused injury to his brain. Jason came out without a scratch. The police gave him a breathalyzer test when they arrived at the scene, then took him down to the station to be urine tested for drugs. He came up positive for cocaine. As per usual, Kim came to the rescue and immediately found him a good lawyer, hoping for the best for both of them.

Jason was shaken to his core. At sentencing, the judge gave him the choice of serving three months' jail time or entering a drug and alcohol rehab center. The judge added a two-year suspension on his license and 200 hours of community service. Mark's "sentence" was worse by far. An MRI showed evidence of permanent damage to the speech center of his brain. Mark sued Jason's insurance company, and their friendship of twenty years ended abruptly.

Jason chose to go through a thirty-day rehab program, something he had always resisted doing. Kim was relieved and waited patiently for Jason to come home a new person. At that point, she had no idea of her own issue with codependency, and was even more unaware of how they played into Jason's addiction.

Six months later, Kim and Jason made an appointment to see me. After everything they had been through, their relationship was barely afloat. Jason's time in rehab had catapulted them into first stage recovery, and they were working to climb toward second stage. Jason met weekly with his outpatient therapist and was working with a sponsor on the 12 steps of AA. (A sponsor is someone who shows a new member how to work the 12 steps, lends a friendly ear, and offers direction.) Kim regularly called a few friends she had met in the family group of Jason's rehab program. Still, the couple were unsure whether it was safe to exhale and trust that sobriety wasn't just a pie-in-the-sky idea.

By the time I met them, Kim and Jason were flirting more with ideas of separation and divorce than with each other. They were scared, anxious, angry, and baffled. They could not understand why their fantasies of what recovery was supposed to bring them were so far removed from the reality they were actually living. They had experienced years of suffering, yo-yoing between overinvolvement with each other and too much alienation. And now this?

Kim said, "Over the last six months, Jason and I have felt so grateful for a second chance at life. But we have still found ourselves bickering and fighting over the littlest things. I just don't get it. Now that Jason is in recovery, why hasn't everything fallen into place like I imagined it would?"

I told them that Jason's getting sober was a huge first step that he needed to take toward improving their situation. I said, "After all you've been through, I'm sure we can agree that Jason staying sober is your best bet for things to get better. However, being sober is not, on its own, enough to make everything magically fall into place. If you want a happy and healthy partnership, you both must be willing to take a deeper look within yourselves and your relationship. This is the only way you will be able to break the fantasy spell that's been cast over you by such culprits as the family and culture in which you grew up—and that you are bringing with you into recovery."

Kim and Jason did this work in the context of therapy. But you can do it by yourself with the following information and exercises.

The Fantasy Spell

Let's start with the fantasy spell that one or both partners can fall under merely by getting into recovery. It is what drives the recovering addict to believe, "Finally! I am free of my addictions, so all the annoying, frustrating, and infuriating things my partner does to me are going to disappear! No more pain and sorrow!" Likewise, it is what causes you as a recovering codependent to believe, "Finally! My partner is addiction-free, so everything is going to fall into place. No more suffering!"

I refer to this as a fantasy spell because it is based on the expectation that problems will simply dissolve, as if through the waving of a magic wand. It is an irrational state of mind that can come over even the smartest people.

This spell played out in Kim and Jason's relationship much like a romantic movie with a very unrealistic plot. As soon as Jason got sober, Kim started creating a movie in her head with Jason in the starring role as the responsible, protective partner. At the same time,

Jason started to imagine Kim in the costarring role as his lighthearted, sexy wife. Perhaps most significantly, neither Kim nor Jason was aware of what they were doing. They didn't realize that they were constantly weighing the reality of their relationship against the fantasy relationship playing out in their minds. The awesome person Kim imagined Jason would become when he got sober looked nothing like the angry, depressed guy sleeping in the bed next to her. Jason, on the other hand, couldn't understand why Kim wasn't readily forgiving him for his past drunken betrayals now that he had committed to sobriety. She didn't match up with the fantasy wife who loved and supported him no matter what. As long as Kim and Jason continued living under their own respective fantasy spells, they each felt the other was coming up short.

TRY THIS: Identify Your Fantasy Spell

If you are like most people in first stage recovery, you are vulnerable to being under a fantasy spell. Can you identify yours? Fill in the blank. You can give as many details as you want to describe your fantasy.

1. My fantasy about my partner is that _____.
   (For example: "My fantasy about my partner is that he is going to be more communicative and loving now that he is in recovery. He will take me out on Saturday nights.")

2. My partner's fantasy about me is that _____.
   (For example: "My partner's fantasy about me is that I'm going to let go of all my resentments now that she has put down her addiction.")

   Note that I'm not asking you to research your partner's fantasy to use as evidence against him or her. Recognizing your own fantasy is not something you should use against yourself, either. What's important here is that you bring into your consciousness the beliefs and ideas you carry that may be hurting you without your even knowing it. You don't want to condemn your relationship because it fails to live up to ideas you've internalized unconsciously. And it goes without saying you don't want your partner to condemn you, either.

At first glance—especially if you are in the early stages of recovery—living under a fantasy spell might seem far easier than delving into uncomfortable psychological and emotional realities. But trust me, it isn't. A fantasy spell stands between you and your recovering partner and prevents either of you from moving into second stage recovery.

Remember, your fantasies may feel very real to you, but the fact is, they're only mental images of what you wish would occur or fear could happen. The positive ones usually have no feelings of anxiety, fear, depression, or anger associated with them. The negative ones do. Either way, they are not reality.

The advantage of using a mindfulness practice here is that you can take your unconscious mind out of the driver's seat and put your aware mind in its place. This helps you recognize not only what your fantasies are, but also how persistently they may have steered you and your relationship in the wrong direction. Perhaps you're thinking, *Wow, I didn't even know my ideas about my partner were fantasies.* But, now you do! The freedom you can give yourself just by connecting the dots with your own aware thinking can be mind-boggling.

MINDFULNESS MEDITATION:
Appreciate Your Relationship

Read these instructions to yourself, then put down the book and do the meditation.

1. Take a moment to sit back in your chair and get comfortable.

2. Close your eyes. Take a deep breath in and a long breath out, and allow yourself to relax.

3. Notice where you are holding tension in your body. Breathe into those places and allow yourself to relax more fully.

4. As you continue mindful breathing, bring to mind the partner you chose to find love and companionship with, whom you fight for and against, and with whom you hope to fulfill your deepest yearnings.

5. Allow yourself to appreciate the heaven and the hell of this path: the good, the bad, and the ugly. As you continue to relax into your breath, appreciate what it means to surrender. You may be in the best place with your partner right now, in the worst, or just coasting on mediocre. Whichever way, let yourself be here now. Here is all we have in any moment.

6. See if you can give yourself the luxury of not knowing and not having to know exactly how or when things are going to get better. Appreciate the luxury of being curious without any expectations about what is to come. For a few moments, see if you can leave your life as it is and be present with yourself.

7. Whenever you are ready, take a deep breath, and open your eyes.

Your Relationship Frame of Reference

One of my jobs with Jason and Kim was to help them break their fantasy spell by facing up to their issues of addiction and codependency. I told them that the first step toward a deeper understanding of their relationship was to examine where the frames of reference they used in romantic relationships came from.

By *frame of reference*, I mean the various feelings and attitudes that you have about relationships and that influence how you act in the present moment with your partner. Your parental upbringing—that is, how your parents related to each other and to you—is one important influence on your frame of reference. Other influences are genetics, learning disabilities, past trauma, mental illness, cultural background, education, and religion. For now, let's stick to the influence of your parental upbringing. We will look at some of these other influences in later chapters.

If you don't know the origin of your frame of reference, chances are you will be blindly ruled by it. This is what psychologists mean when they refer to the "power of the unconscious." The *unconscious* is all the stuff you hold in your mind that has a party in your dreams while you sleep each night, and makes the decisions you later don't know why you made. The unconscious is what can make you confused about why you chose your partner, why you took your career path, and why you have the friends you have. You know the conscious factors that inform your choices, but your conscious mind is never the whole picture. Your unconscious is at play and is seeking ways to make itself known to you through the many life choices you make.

Hyperpositive and *hypernegative* are the two most common frames of reference held by the codependent and the addict. If your parents were overly indulgent and avoided conflict, your frame of reference for relationships will tend toward being *hyperpositive*. If they were neglectful, harsh, or abusive, it will tend toward being *hypernegative*. Of course, not every child was either overly protected from the difficult realities of life or abused and neglected. You may find yourself somewhere between these extremes.

Let's look at each of the two types more closely. Some individuals developed a hyperpositive frame of reference because they were never allowed to see their parents fight or disagree with each other. These parents would say just about anything to avoid causing their children disappointment and suffering. If you aren't sure you recognize this style, watch a few episodes of 1950s shows, such as *Leave It to Beaver* or *Ozzie and Harriet*. You'll see that Mom and Dad were very nice people who slept in twin beds and never had grown-up talk with their kids about anything beyond the birds and the bees. This kind of parenting creates a frame of reference filled with unrealistic notions of life and romance. Certainly, the individuals raised by such parents are unprepared for the big bumps in the road and frustrations that life and real relationships bring. It's no wonder they are hugely disappointed, shocked, and angry at what the real deal doles out.

Other individuals developed a hypernegative frame of reference for partnership from watching their parents be abusive, disrespectful, and unloving toward each other. They grew used to their parents' aggressive behavior, unpredictable mood swings, and lack of support for them. They may have experienced serious neglect and indifference from their parents. These people can develop a wildly high tolerance for or sensitivity to suffering and deprivation. They might not know when to put their foot down with their partner, or else become abusive themselves. They could recreate what I call "the familiar horrible" and end up in an abusive relationship, or decide to never again be with anyone who acts like either of their parents. Some of these people have an incredibly high tolerance for neglect; others, conversely, have a zero tolerance policy for their partner's bad behavior because, to them, "where there's smoke, there's fire." This is a problem because, to be in a long-term relationship with a real person, you must be able to put up with normal levels of anger and frustration coming from your partner. So if you have a history of abuse, or your parents were abusive to each other, things can become very complicated when examining your frame of reference and how it has ruled your choices in your romantic life.

The following table shows typical feelings and attitudes expressed by partners with different frames of reference for relationships. See if you recognize yourself in either group.

Hyperpositive	Hypernegative
It's realistic to expect my partner to know me better than I know myself.	Deep down I'm sure my partner doesn't really love me.
I'm not the one who has to change. Just my staying in the relationship is enough.	I don't trust I'll ever be completely safe with my partner.
My partner never does enough to make things work for us.	Happiness is for other people, not me.
I'm sure there's a partner out there who'd be happy to meet my needs. I just haven't found him/her yet.	My partner always thinks I'm not doing enough to make things work for us.
I have to remind my partner something is wrong with him or her.	My partner feels there is someone out there who'd make him/her happier than I do.
I'm much easier to get along with than my partner is.	My partner always says something is wrong with me.
I don't understand why my partner says no to anything I ask for.	I'm afraid to ask for more from my partner.
I don't want to give my partner half as much attention as he or she asks for.	I will do anything to make sure my partner doesn't get mad at me.
My partner should be understanding when I hurt his or her feelings. Obviously, it's not my intention.	Some part of me is afraid that I'm not good enough for my partner.
What's wrong with expecting my partner to sacrifice his or her needs for my happiness?	I avoid conflict with my partner, even if I lose out as a result.

After investigating their own backgrounds, Kim and Jason were able to uncover their respective frames of reference.

Kim's parents were both alcoholics, and although they remained married, their family life was marked by frequent fights, during which neither parent had the energy to attend to Kim or her younger sister. As a result, Kim felt responsible for taking care of her sister and also for looking after her mother, who was prone to bouts with depression. The hypernegative frame of reference she brought to her marriage with Jason included the expectation that a partner was supposed to be a burden with needs that mattered more than her own. In her fantasy, Kim saw Jason's recovery as the key to turning him into the partner who would love her unconditionally and give her the attention she had so longed for as a child. Finally she was going to create a relationship that had no resemblance to her parents'. When Jason failed to live up to that fantasy and instead continued to present his own set of needs and demands, she felt despondent and confused.

Jason and his twin brother were raised by their mother alone after their father died of a heart attack when the boys were twelve years old. Jason said his parents adored each other, and he had never seen them in conflict. His mother never remarried. He described his mother as a saint. She took care of Jason by giving him anything and everything he asked for, and she tried hard to be his best friend. He was allowed to drink at home, had friends over any time he wanted, and wasn't expected to help with household chores. Losing his father at an early age, and being left with an idealized vision of his parents' marriage, led Jason to develop a hyperpositive frame of reference. Unbeknownst to him, he expected Kim to become his protector, much like his indulgent mother.

So, what about your frame of reference?

TRY THIS: Identify Your Frame of Reference

To help you identify your frame of reference, based on your upbringing, I have compiled three sets of statements. Take a few minutes to read these lists and check off those statements with which you most identify.

List #1

_____ *Your parents were very protective of you.*

_____ *You could do no wrong in your parents' eyes. Your parents praised you whether you were working hard or not.*

_____ *Your parents didn't have the heart to say no to anything you wanted.*

_____ *Your parents could not stand to see you go through anything that made you suffer, and they were always there to soothe your feelings.*

_____ *You can't remember if you were ever punished for anything that you did wrong.*

_____ *You talk to your mother, or your father, almost every day. You don't mind it because it makes them happy.*

_____ *Your parents had a very hard time keeping their opinions to themselves if they did not like the person in whom you had a romantic interest.*

_____ *You never saw your parents fight.*

_____ *You sometimes felt smothered by your parents' love for you.*

_____ *Your parents insisted on talking with your friends whenever they came over.*

_____ *Your parents rescued you from having to suffer the consequences of the mistakes you made, big or small.*

_____ *You don't know what you would do without your parents' financial help or emotional guidance.*

List #2

_____ *You felt afraid of your parents.*

_____ *Your parents hit you.*

_____ *You stopped talking to your parents after you moved away from home.*

_____ *You're not sure if your parents liked each other.*

_____ *Your mother only gave you affection when you were sick.*

_____ *You always wanted your friends to adopt you into their families.*

_____ *Going home to your family causes you great anxiety.*

_____ *You did not like to bring friends home.*

_____ *You did not feel liked by your parents much of the time.*

_____ *You never felt the way your parents punished your siblings and you was appropriate to the actual things you did wrong.*

_____ *You felt neglected by your parents.*

_____ *You hid in your room a lot.*

List #3

_____ *Your parents let you use them as your backbone until you could stand on your own two feet.*

_____ *Your parents were extremely proud of your accomplishments, your interests, and the life choices you made.*

_____ *Your parents tried both to shelter you from suffering and to open your eyes to the suffering of the world you lived in.*

_____ *When you worked hard to succeed at what you pursued, your parents rewarded you with the things you wanted.*

_____ *You grew up loving family gatherings, especially during the holidays.*

_____ *You speak to your parents regularly, not because you have to, but because you want to.*

_____ *Your parents have always had a balanced perspective on you. They know what you're good at and what you're weak at, and helped you with both.*

_____ *Your parents were affectionate to each other and toward you.*

_____ *You rarely saw your parents fight, but when they did, it was more like a strong discussion. Any yelling there was didn't last long.*

_____ *As much as you hated it, your parents gave you consequences when you deserved them. And in your heart you knew they were right.*

_____ *Your parents trusted your choices of people you were romantically interested in.*

_____ *You loved having your friends over at your house.*

If you checked mainly statements in the first list, your frame of reference may be hyperpositive. If you checked mainly statements in the second list, your frame of reference may be hypernegative. If you checked mainly statements in the third list, your frame of reference may be balanced and middle of the road, similar to that of most people who don't struggle with addiction or codependency. I say "may" because this exercise is meant merely to serve as a rough guide and (like other exercises in this book) should not be seen as a foolproof test.

The New Normal of Recovery

When I first met Kim, she said, "I'm just looking for a normal life. I just want to be with someone I can trust and feel safe with."

Jason said, "I just want Kim to forgive me and life to be more fun."

Both of them were driven by their fantasies, which they felt should be more easily attainable. The hyperpositive and hypernegative frames of reference they brought to the table didn't help, either. They wanted a normal relationship, but they hadn't yet learned to distinguish between their fantasies and reality.

It is unrealistic for anyone newly free of addiction or codependency to expect to get the normal relationship they want by just stepping onto the playing field of recovery. They aren't going to suddenly morph into a stable, connected, passionate, and mindful couple. Some hard work is required. The new normal is earned over time, and not by waving a magic wand of fantasy over your relationship.

It was now time for a healthy dose of tough love. I told Jason and Kim, "No more fairy tales. Now you are living in the world of recovering partners—learning to tolerate normal amounts of frustration and to break the spells that were cast over you. Times of conflict and feelings of estrangement are normal in any close relationship, and are to be expected when you love someone who is in recovery. The closest thing to living happily ever after in the real world of recovery is to experience an upward trend of feeling better and better over time."

Jason and Kim both breathed a sigh of relief. They said it was nice not to have to pretend to be in better shape than they were, and to know they were more like other couples on the path to recovery than they had thought. They were eager to do whatever it took to get better acquainted with their new normal.

Clarifying Your Values

I told Jason and Kim that now that they were more accountable for the fantasies they brought to their relationship, the next step was for them to evaluate the influence of their value systems. On a day-to-day basis, your value system determines your experience of compatibility with your recovering partner. If you want to understand why you feel aligned with your partner and why you two fight about the things you do, you need only look as far as your value systems.

Let's start with a simple example. Suppose your top value in life is self-actualization, and your recovering partner's is travel. In this case, you may feel rejected if your partner prefers to explore the Amazon rather than join you on a month-long meditation retreat. Before assuming your partner doesn't respect you, or love you as much as you love him or her, consider whether you are operating from disparate priorities. Your recovering partner may also value self-actualization and want to share related activities, but this may not be his or her top value.

TRY THIS: Explore Your Values

1. To begin to clarify your values, make a list that includes all the things you hold in high esteem. The following are examples of core values that many people carry. You can use these as a starting point, but make sure your list reflects your own personal priorities.

   - Novelty, adventure, spontaneity, risk

   - Security, predictability, comfort

   - Being of service to others

   - Personal transformation and growth

- Connection, intimacy

- Higher education, being a lifelong learner

- Significance in the world, fame, recognition

- Spirituality, religion, God, faith

- Sexuality

- Children, being a parent

- Creativity, art, music, poetry, dance

- Friends

- Making money

- Physical health, athletics

- Travel

- Politics

2. Now rank the items on your list in order of their importance, from the most to the least important. Keep in mind that this is the order of importance for you as of today. What you hold in top priority today may not be what you hold in top priority at a future date.

3. Ask if your recovering partner would like to explore his or her value system and discuss how your respective values compare. If your partner isn't interested at this time, no worries! You can become the secret change agent in your relationship. In other words, you bring to the table whatever you learn about yourself, whether your partner knows it or not. As you shine the spotlight on your own values, it may become clear to you that some of the fights you have are simply because of differences in priority—they don't reflect any fundamental lack of love or respect between the two of you.

Cultivating Acceptance

Jason and Kim continued to have conversations together about what they could realistically expect from each other and how their value systems matched up. Kim talked about what it would mean to have a partner she trusted and felt safe with. Jason expressed what it would take to have more fun together. They discussed how their upbringing influenced how they had been relating to each other and how they could be more generous in considering what the other valued. They shared their fantasies of each other and worked together to sort out what was pure fantasy and what actually could be achieved.

Acceptance was a key ingredient in this process. This included Kim's acceptance of herself as a recovering codependent, as well as her acceptance of Jason as a recovering addict. It also included acceptance of all aspects of their recovery process together. In fact, acceptance is a starting point. Like Jason and Kim, you are going to have to start by accepting that it will take time and effort to break the spell of your own fantasies. It will take time and effort to shift your frame of reference from hyperpositive or hypernegative to being mindfully present with your experience and not getting swept up in old ideas. To foster acceptance, I had Jason and Kim do the following mindfulness meditation. You can do it, too.

MINDFULNESS MEDITATION:
Accept Yourself

Read these instructions to yourself, then put down the book and do the meditation.

1. Take a moment to sit back in your chair and get comfortable.

2. Close your eyes. Begin to tune in to the sensations in your body, as well as to your emotional state.

3. Let go of any idea that you need to do anything right now, other than saying to yourself, "I accept me. I accept all of me."

4. As you follow your breath in and out, keep repeating this statement silently to yourself.

5. Allow yourself to feel appreciation for all the efforts you are making to be in alignment with the reality of your life as it is today.

6. Take a moment to be proud of your stamina and commitment to finding out who you are without the past programming of your historical frame of reference.

7. Enjoy the idea of washing away old ideas and bringing in new ones.

8. Before you open your eyes, take a few more mindful breaths and say to yourself three more times, "I accept me. I accept all of me."

TRY THIS: Find a New Normal

Acceptance is the foundation from which you and your partner can build your new normal and begin to explore your respective frames of reference and value systems. This exercise includes some questions to ask your partner to help launch a discussion about your partner's upbringing and how those past experiences might inform who he or she is today. Don't approach this discussion in a way that makes your partner think you've gone off the deep end and are trying to play shrink. Rather, do it in a natural and casual way. Explain that you are wondering about these things because you have been reading this book.

Again, if your partner isn't game for this sort of conversation, that is fine—you go right ahead and reword these questions for yourself. The more clarity you have in your own mind about who you are, the more clarity you will bring to your relationship. So don't worry if your partner isn't ready to play this mental parlor game. You are still going to be a change agent for your relationship, whether your partner knows it or not!

Here are the questions:

- *What do you recall most vividly about your upbringing?*

- *What obvious messages about relationships did you get from your parents?*

- *What unspoken messages did you get from your parents?*

- *How has your upbringing affected how you are in our relationship?*

- *How does your upbringing affect your expectations of me and our relationship?*

- *How do you think my upbringing affects my expectations of you and our relationship?*

- *How did your parents negotiate any differences in their values?*

If your partner is open to talking, be careful with these kinds of conversations. Tread lightly. You may be jumping for joy that I've given you license to talk with your partner about how his or her parents are to blame for the negative ways that he or she has acted toward you or the unrealistic expectations he or she holds. The name of this exercise isn't The Blame Game! Its purpose is to open up conversation so that the two of you can develop a greater awareness of each other and can reconnect at a deeper level. If you aren't ready yet to do this in the spirit in which it is intended, hold off. Better to wait and do it in the future than to try now and run aground.

Even if you do approach this conversation in the intended spirit, it may not go smoothly. One or both of you may get heated. Or you may end up feeling distant. Remember, this is all par for the course. And it's not just about one conversation. You can repeat this exercise as often as you want. I invite you to come up with new questions of your own.

Finally, here is an exercise I gave Jason and Kim to help them get back on track and feel less distant from each other. It is an exercise that works especially well for partners navigating the obstacles that may arise when they begin to explore deeper issues together. I told them it was a homework assignment that was nonnegotiable. In other words, I wanted Jason and Kim to agree to do this, even if they weren't always feeling in the mood. They said they were game.

TRY THIS: Start a Mindfulness Hugging Routine

This is something you can do right now that will get you moving toward a daily dose of closeness with your partner.

You probably don't leave your house in the morning without saying good-bye to your kids. You probably don't neglect kissing them hello when you come home, either. It may not occur to you that it is equally as important to do the same with your recovering partner. You may think, "I am an adult now; I'm done doing the heavy lifting with my partner. It's my turn to come and go as I please." Or "I am so busy trying to get everything on my plate done each day that I don't even have a moment to hug my partner." Even the simplest daily expressions of emotional manners, such as hugging hello and good-bye, may have gone out the window by the time your partner finally got into recovery.

Start a daily hugging routine today. It may seem obvious how to hug your partner, but when you are adding mindfulness to the mix, it gets a little more technical. Follow these steps:

1. Stand face to face with your partner, with your heads crooked in each other's necks.

2. Wrap one, or both, arms around your partner's shoulder. If you use only one arm, wrap the other around your partner's waist.

3. Feel your body connecting with your partner's.

4. Allow whatever thoughts and feelings you have to be there, and take the time you need to find peace in your heart and a relaxed body posture.

5. Continue to hold each other until you feel completely relaxed. Do not let go until you have reached a mutual state of relaxation.

Note that this is not intended to be a sexual exercise. But it can make being close to your partner seem like a safe and comforting harbor—whether it's one you used to enjoy or one you never fully experienced before. By the time you get to chapter 6, "Intimacy and Desire," you may find you've made headway in your sex life with this kind of daily practice.

In fact, hugging is an important aspect of mindfulness on your path to recovery. While you're hugging, you and your partner will be focused on the present moment. You'll be practicing acceptance and not judging each other, while generating mutual heartfelt warmth. I'll bet you didn't realize mindfulness could be so warm and fuzzy!

Conclusion

If you've made it to the end of this chapter and followed through on the suggested exercises, it is a safe bet you've done the work to start breaking your own fantasy spells. Hopefully, you have attempted to warm things up a little with the simple gesture of hugging, as well.

As you continue to shake off all the alluring but false fairy tales your mother used to read you, and in their place create a new, mindful frame of reference for your relationship, your brain will get adjusted to your new normal. For those of you who came from the opposite type of fairy-tale upbringing, the same goes for you. Not every potential partner is really an abuser in disguise. And hopefully the recovering partner you have right now isn't, either. Those only existed in the Grimms' fairy tales you grew up with.

I wouldn't be surprised if you said right now that your brain is feeling a little taxed from all this figuring things out. That's okay. Just see it as a mental workout and give yourself a gold star for hanging in there and taking the time to deepen your understanding of yourself.

CHAPTER 3

Establishing and Maintaining Boundaries: Getting to Know Yourself

"Now that my boyfriend is sober, I want to stay on the top of a mountain alone with him and never come down!" So said Angie, thirty-two years old. Although her comment may sound sweet to some, it exposes how dangerous the prospect of learning to create boundaries can feel for codependents once their partner gets on a recovering path. That prospect felt threatening to her boyfriend, too. Being entwined had historically defined them as a couple. Although painful and unsatisfying, it was their security and their oxygen.

When I suggested taking steps out into the world on her own, Angie's focus was still on trying to hold on to the comfort and security she and her boyfriend had created for themselves. She didn't realize that satisfying her yearning would do nothing to actualize their relationship. This is common among codependents.

As a recovering codependent, you must resist the temptation to remain overly entangled with your partner. Instead, the goal is to be mindful in setting new personal boundaries and bolstering autonomy. If you haven't already become clear about where you start and end in relationship to your partner, this chapter will help you do that. The questions and exercises will lead you through a process of clarifying how you became overly entangled, how you can rediscover your identity, and how you can make all this work within your relationship. For starters, though, just know that for any relationship to bring out the best in both parties, there have to be clear-cut limits, or boundaries, in place. Even the dog you love isn't allowed to jump up on the dinner table and eat off of your plate, right?

Where It All Begins...

Remember when you and your partner came together as two separate individuals? You had a desire for romance and put your best foot forward when you started dating. You wanted your top qualities to shine, just as you would in a job interview, except you wanted to end up in the bedroom and not the boardroom. I'm not saying there is anything wrong with this. You did it. I did it. We all do it. It is human nature to want love, connection, and partnership.

Nevertheless, even on a very first date, people pick up on each other's nonverbal cues, subtle vibes, facial expressions, and simple gestures—all those signs that reveal what is going on beneath the surface. Like most people, you probably knew better than to jump at every nuance you noticed on that first date. You didn't say, "So, you're not keeping eye contact with me when I ask you questions about yourself. Why is that?" You're equally unlikely to offer up, "Let me tell you about me. You may not be able to tell by the confident way I look and speak that I'm really an anxious caretaker." Not only would that take the joy and spontaneity out of any date, it would also seem really weird.

People embarking on a new relationship may silently reassure themselves that they must be wrong about any incongruent cues they picked up, and tell themselves they are just being hypersensitive. Again, you probably did this, too. Certainly, no one wants to be judgmental or rude coming out of the gate, especially if he or she feels some chemistry and is hoping for a second date.

The feeling between two people can be so mesmerizing it eclipses any red flags. The intense passion makes people unwittingly say good-bye to their boundaries and throw their mental checklist for their perfect partner out the window. We call this the *honeymoon phase* of a relationship. It can last as little as a few weeks or go on for many months. During this phase, the brain is hyperfocused on its new object of desire, and thus ignores any danger signals or warning signs.

You may have forgotten what the honeymoon phase felt like for you and your recovering partner. May I refresh your memory? There you were, confident in your own identity, knowing who you were and who you weren't. Then along came your partner, who royally rang your chimes. You fell asleep thinking about your partner and woke up thinking about him or her, too. You had boundless energy and sexuality and made time for endless conversations. You suddenly couldn't remember what life had been like the day before you met and were thrust into a world where you thought like a "we" and not like a "me."

During the honeymoon phase, you were nice, excited, and endlessly curious about your new love interest. Compassion and appreciation were your middle names. You cried over what your partner cried over and swooned over the smallest kindnesses. You found yourself picking up your partner's tastes: for example, you never liked camping, but because your new love did, suddenly you were not only camping but taking courses on wilderness survival. It was a magical time when your relationship reigned supreme. Are things starting to come back to you?

...And Where It's All Headed

For codependents who get involved with addicts, the honeymoon phase is likely to come to a premature halt. Whether or not the addict is actively in addiction when love first blooms, the bliss of connection will soon be accompanied by unpredictable behaviors, moodiness, or broken promises. Rather than making a beeline for the nearest exit at these signs, as other partners might, a codependent typically responds by gripping more tightly to the addict partner, going into denial, or being unreasonably accommodating.

The disease of addiction always turns a relationship toward disaster because it inhibits the development of a balance between your and your partner's individual identities and the identity of the relationship. When the honeymoon phase comes to a halt, the addict and the codependent continue to cling to each other. They both fail to mature because they don't establish boundaries that support their individual autonomy—that is, their sense of independent selfhood. Instead, they monopolize each other's time, let go of other friendships, become barometers of each other's emotions, and glue themselves together. As a result, by the time your partner gets into recovery, you have pretty much lost your sense of how to establish boundaries with each other.

Just as the bliss that came with the honeymoon phase at the beginning of your relationship faded, so too will the thrill that comes at the beginning of recovery. It is common to assume that, in both cases, one's relationship will naturally and seamlessly transition into a new phase. Not true for the addict and the codependent! They keep hanging on for dear life. Instead of learning to relate within a framework of healthy boundaries, they become what psychologists term *enmeshed*.

The process of finding your own autonomy from your recovering partner requires that you deal with your boundary issues head-on. Simply put, you make the decision to stop ignoring all those darn red flags and instead start to mindfully listen to what your instincts are telling you. You allow your instincts to guide you in establishing meaningful boundaries that build a foundation of trust and security not only within yourself, but within your partnership, as well. This can be as simple as knowing and respecting the times when you feel threatened and need to lean away, and taking the right actions to support those feelings. Or knowing when you feel safe enough to lean into your partner, and doing that instead. Of course, all this can feel confusing and complicated at first, but gradually you will come to terms with how much you are willing to sacrifice to make your relationship work, and how much you will refuse to give up. You may not have identified your boundaries in relationship to your recovering partner before, but there has never been a better time than now.

Question: "Why Do I Need a More Separate Life from My Recovering Partner? Aren't We Supposed to Work Out Our Relationship Struggles Together?"

Meet Alison. Her girlfriend, Samantha, had been in recovery from drug and alcohol abuse for nine months when Alison practically dragged her to therapy. She began by unloading her resentments. "I've been an amazing girlfriend to Samantha since day one, and I feel completely unappreciated. I never stopped doing everything I could to support her while she was getting loaded, and have continued to since she got sober. I made excuses for her behavior to her friends and family; paid bills she couldn't afford; and please, on top of that, I was always the designated driver. I wasn't her girlfriend, I was her slave.

We need to be able to talk about our problems together now that she is sober. But instead of spending time with me, she runs out to meetings or spends hours whispering on the phone with her sponsor. I feel like she doesn't need me anymore."

So far, Samantha had not said one word. She just sat there looking annoyed and frustrated. I turned to her and asked, "Can you understand why Alison is feeling so hurt by you?"

She said, "Of course. She thinks she's the perfect angel because she's been taking care of me all these years. I never asked her to do that; she chose it. I didn't get sober to have someone watch over my every move. And I didn't get sober to have someone nag at me for being too involved with AA. I feel like I can't win. Alison went crazy when I was drinking and using, and now she is going crazy that I'm sober! I love Alison, but she needs to get a life that doesn't revolve around me all the time!"

Alison looked wilted. She had yet to understand that her girlfriend wasn't the only one in the relationship who needed to make some changes. She didn't know it was time to do a little soul searching of her own. She asked, "Why do I need a more separate life from my recovering partner? I'm confused. Aren't we supposed to work out our relationship struggles together?"

For the record, this is one of the questions I've heard most frequently from codependents over the years. Every significant phase of growth may be accompanied by strong moments of confusion and self-doubt. You may not be sure you can tolerate the rigor of carving out your independence from your recovering partner, especially if you felt lonely and neglected for a long time before your partner got into recovery.

Listen. It's normal to be confused. In fact, it's to be expected. Let's look at the two interrelated parts to Alison's question: why creating boundaries is important, and how those boundaries affect relationship issues.

Resist the Temptation to Stay Enmeshed

You may question the need for a more separate life from your recovering partner for a number of reasons—out of habit, fear, or misguided ideas about what makes for a good relationship. You may be used to following the rules of enmeshment but overlook the negative repercussions. Yet, like Alison, you probably "know in your heart" that greater separation is needed in your relationship. So the question is how you can achieve that separation without being burdened by too much stress or anxiety.

To begin with, I think it's fair to say that once your partner gets into recovery, you can expect to feel befuddled. You may fluctuate between feeling anxiety and guilt for being what you feel is too independent from him or her and concern and unease about what seems like too much independence on his or her part. As you start to see the value of independence, you may feel ashamed of just how much dependency you want, how much you still want your partner to depend on you. Facing these quandaries head-on can be uncomfortable, and you may find yourself fighting to stay enmeshed just to avoid the bad feelings that arise from these attempts at autonomy.

This is where mindfulness comes in. Perhaps I've mistakenly given you the impression that mindfulness is mainly a matter of sitting around with your eyes closed. If so, let's correct that now. Remember the three practices I introduced in chapter 1? Now is the time to focus on the one that says *The Key to Change Rests in the Present Moment*. One way to move in the direction of greater autonomy is to find activities you enjoy doing on a regular basis outside your relationship. This is one way to practice mindfulness with your eyes wide open.

TRY THIS: Engage Mindfully in a Hobby

The objective of first stage recovery from codependency is to redefine and sustain your separate identity, not just in times of stress, but as a part of your way of life. Finding a hobby with the intention of enhancing your autonomy will not only cultivate your enjoyment of being by yourself, but also make separating from your recovering partner when needed feel less threatening. It can be something as simple as pursuing a hobby you haven't had time for, either because you were caught in the web of your partner's active addiction or because you were overly involved with his or her recovery.

I say "engage mindfully" in a hobby because this is not an activity you are taking up as a means of escape, a way to strike out against your partner, or anything of that sort. It is a positive engagement for yourself. It is not a buffer against anything; rather, it is a means for gaining the strong backbone you'll need to set and maintain new boundaries. The outside interests you mindfully pursue will build strength against the gravitational pull toward enmeshment with your partner. Your hobbies will become your best friends and make you feel more well-rounded, interesting, and confident as an individual. Here are a few examples of hobbies you can take up:

Piano	Hiking	Fishing
Salsa	Bicycling	Skiing
Toastmasters	Painting	Bowling
Poetry writing	Stamp or coin collecting	Party planning
Bridge	Cooking	Needlepoint
Book club	Tennis	Crossword puzzles
Poker	Gardening	Horseback riding
Golf	Bird watching	Swimming
Knitting	Volunteer work	Photography

The list goes on and on. I could keep coming up with ideas, but I might lead you to join a club or take a class you wouldn't enjoy. So pick one of your own, and just do it!

You may find that breaking out of your daily rhythm and adding new activities is difficult, especially if you have been trapped in fear and unable to take your eyes off your partner. If that is the case, before you go to sleep tonight, allow yourself to wander around in your imagination. Think of the things you loved doing as a child or things you have seen other people do that sparked your interest. Let your imagination guide you in revisiting old hobbies or in picking up new ones. Give yourself the freedom to dabble in various hobbies before you land on something that really absorbs your attention and brings passion to your life.

Know When to Step Away and When to Step Closer

Recognizing the value of being more separate allows you to take actions, such as starting a hobby, on your own behalf. But what does this mean for your relationship? Alison expressed concern that creating greater separation would make it more difficult for her and Samantha to work on their relationship.

This is a frequent misconception among codependents. Enmeshment gives codependents the feeling of being less alone in the world. It preserves the illusion of protection from abandonment. Even though they really want to find their own sense of themselves, codependents often end up staying enmeshed with their recovering partner for this reason.

Alison had no idea how to differentiate between boundaries that were a sign of the relationship deteriorating and boundaries that would bring hearty autonomy to the relationship. As a result, she continued to tailgate her recovering girlfriend and avoided figuring things out for herself, even though the struggle to sustain enmeshment with Samantha only led to constant anxiety, frustration, and fear.

This kind of enmeshment is called a *double bind*. Basically, you're damned if you do and damned if you don't. It's painful to be enmeshed. But it is also painful to be in limbo, separate from your partner. This type of double bind is one of the reasons many codependents alternate between clinging to their partner as one would to a life preserver and trying to escape the relationship as if it were the bubonic plague.

You are not alone in this double bind. Both you and your recovering partner have major concerns about getting to know each other as separate people. You may have been living as if your relationship was more important than your own life for as long as you've been with your partner. Please know that your recovering partner will be just as confused. Your partner has let you run the show for so long, or hidden from your control, that the word "boundary" isn't in his or her vocabulary either. This news may help you relax a bit. But perhaps, like Alison and Samantha, you're still feeling bewildered. Codependents and the partners they love both need concrete ways to assert boundaries without setting each other off emotionally. One extremely helpful technique for this is a technique I like to call the mindful walk-away.

I said to Alison, "I realize it can feel very confusing when you don't know whether to soothe your own anxieties or rely on Samantha to help you. I am going to teach you an exercise I call the mindful walk-away. It's a great way to disconnect from any of Samantha's behaviors that leave you with the impulse to beg, cajole, or chase her. Of course, you both are free to use this exercise. The most important ground rule, though, is that you both have to agree that the other has permission to use it. Okay?"

They both agreed.

TRY THIS: The Mindful Walk-Away

The mindful walk-away is a technique you can use when a conversation is getting too heated and you feel the need to loosen the grip of enmeshment by asserting a boundary. Perhaps most importantly, the mindful walk-away ensures that aggression is not given any place in your relationship. It can be so easy for aggression to come banging on the door of your relationship like a kid on Halloween demanding, "Trick or treat!" Nope, aggression is no longer allowed in your neighborhood.

1. A mindful walk-away is done with kindness. Provided you and your partner have agreed to it ahead of time, either one of you can interrupt and say, "I'm sorry, but this is the time that I need to do a mindful walk-away!"

2. When needed, walk away until you feel you are back in a state of receptivity and ready to reconnect with your partner. Typically, this takes at least twenty minutes. A mindful walk-away can last up to three to six hours, but I don't suggest going longer than that.

3. When a mindful walk-away is called by you or your partner, you might want do a little mindful meditation by sitting down and following your breath and watching your mind and your feelings. But there are no prescriptions here. If running around in circles is what will calm your anxiety about separation in that moment, then do that. If you need to go out to the movies to calm down, do that. Do whatever it takes to tolerate the sudden disengagement. Whatever you choose to do, choose to do it with mindful awareness and remember to breathe, breathe, breathe. Again, a mindful walk-away is only a temporary cooling-off period.

4. When the mindful walk-away is over, you have a chance to come back together and reunite with a cooler head.

The wonderful thing about mindfulness is that it can be done at any time, anywhere, and in any circumstance. Don't be surprised if you find yourselves having to use this technique many times a day until you get the rhythm and can tolerate the new boundaries and the greater spirit of independence you are working to establish.

Note that couples who simply flee from each other in the midst of conflict, without prior agreement or without stating what they are doing, are using walking away as a weapon or as a means of showing callousness. Obviously, I'm not suggesting you use this technique for either of these reasons.

I can't stress enough the value of knowing how to interrupt conversations with your partner before they become hurtful. Most people would agree it is the right of every person to disengage from what is upsetting his or her nervous system, including a partner. Of course, once your nervous system has been set off like a bottle rocket, this is easier to say than to do. So, if you are going to get to where you want to be in your relationship—which I'm assuming is the land of solid interdependence—then the mindful walk-away must become your new best friend. The more you practice it, the more skillful your responses will be during the critical moments when a mindful walk-away makes sense.

You may not be in the habit of tearing yourself away from negative engagement in your relationship. Please note: that is a symptom of codependency. You would rather either cling tightly or put on your emotional boxing gloves and come out swinging than tear yourself away. After all, in your eyes, the engagement may be painful, but at least it's still some kind of engagement. And that can feel better than the loneliness that comes with walking away. But we're on a mission here, right? Know that when you refuse to give in to these habits, they will weaken over time and eventually be completely extinguished. It is the same principle as not adding fuel to a fire so that it will slowly burn itself out.

The Top Thirty Moves That Justify a Mindful Walk-Away

The mindful walk-away is a tool to help preserve your soundness of mind and sense of well-being and to strengthen your sense of autonomy. It will be even more effective if you can begin to recognize the reasons you need to walk away from your partner in the first place. If you aren't clear about when to use the walk-away, consider the following reasons.

RESPECTING YOUR PARTNER'S BOUNDARIES:

Your partner asks you to give him or her some space.

Your partner tells you he or she is feeling overwhelmed by you.

Your partner tells you he or she doesn't feel like talking.

Your partner tells you he or she wants to be alone.

Your partner wants to leave the house without you.

Your partner asks you to stop talking during a conversation.

Your partner tells you he or she feels pressured or bullied by you.

Your partner needs to make a phone call.

Your partner needs to go take a nap.

Your partner wants to meet a friend, go to a meeting, exercise, relax, read, or meditate without you.

RESPECTING YOUR OWN BOUNDARIES:

Your partner starts to bully you.

Your partner won't let you get a word in edgewise.

Your partner shuts down any efforts to have a conversation.

Your partner starts sulking and frowning as you speak to him or her.

Your partner starts to throw the past in your face.

Your partner rolls his or her eyes as you speak.

Your partner starts mocking you as you speak.

Your partner starts to ignore you as you speak.

Your partner starts to humor you condescendingly.

Your partner starts to act confused at *whatever* you say.

Your partner starts accusing you of being oversensitive or touchy.

Your partner starts accusing you of being controlling.

Your partner starts to throw a tantrum.

Your partner starts to threaten to break up.

Your partner starts to beg you never to leave.

Your partner keeps changing the subject.

Your partner starts laughing in your face.

Your partner starts accusing you falsely.

Your partner starts to throw objects against a wall.

You partner starts abusing you psychologically, emotionally, or physically.

You may have gone along with these behaviors without a second thought before recovery. Now that your partner is in recovery and you are taking the bull by the horns and addressing your codependency, you no longer have to tolerate any behaviors that make you feel bad. And your partner can be empowered in the same way!

TRY THIS: Identify What Justifies a Mindful Walk-Away

Instituting polite boundaries and practicing good emotional manners fosters a feeling of safety in any relationship. Even if walking away from your partner or allowing your partner to walk away from you feels as hard as holding hot coals in your hands at first, you will grow calluses from doing it. You will feel proud of your efforts when you become good at this, and it will help you become grade-A relationship material.

1. Make a list of the specific behaviors that would touch off your need to use a mindful walk-away from your partner. Use the thirty reasons I just gave you as a guide.

2. Make a second list of your own specific behaviors that might touch off your partner's need to use a mindful walk-away from you. If possible, consult your partner about this and see how similar or different your lists are.

When you do happen to revert to old, counterproductive behavior, it is most helpful to simply view it as an emotional slip-up and not as proof you are a bad person. Everyone reverts to old behaviors from time to time, and you can't expect to hit the bull's eye 100 percent of the time. What's important is that you have a way to get back on the right path.

Standing in Your Individuality

During the time between being enmeshed with your partner and beginning to stand on your own two feet, it may feel as if love and care have all but disappeared. You may feel isolated and emotionally disconnected; it may seem as if your recovering partner is more like your roommate than your lover. If you can tolerate your separation anxiety and withstand the urge to collapse back into your old ways, you will come to enjoy the benefits autonomy offers. You will be more secure within yourself and with your partner. You will breathe more easily and create room for a connection that is based on love and not fear. You may even start feeling more sexual desire for your partner. If you make a pact with yourself to tolerate the threatening feelings of separateness, paradoxically you will end up coming together in more mature and loving ways. This is not only a promise, it is a prediction.

A lack of clarity about boundaries may leave you confused about what you are entitled to know about your recovering partner's life and what he or she is entitled to keep private from you. This is one of the reasons you might feel tempted to check your partner's e-mail, hire a private investigator, enlist family members to gang up on your partner, or yell through the bathroom door without a second thought. If you insist on behaving like that, your recovering partner may be tempted to join the witness protection program just to get away!

Codependents want to ask their recovering partners all kinds of questions that, for the most part, are not their business to ask, such as "When was the last time you talked to your mother?"—or if their partner is in a 12-step program, "When was the last time you talked to your sponsor?" Or "Who were you on the phone with earlier?" Or "Did you share in your meeting?" Or "What do you tell your friends about me?" "Who are you e-mailing, texting, or talking to?" "Why are you doing (fill in the blank), rather than (fill in the blank)?" I'm sure you get the picture.

Until boundaries are set and rules are made clear, you may remain under the impression that you have unlimited rights to your partner's body, mind, and emotions, and to know where your partner goes; what he or she is doing; and with whom he or she is doing it. You may not perceive what you are doing as annoying or invasive, but your recovering partner probably does!

Ultimately, knowing how to bring calm to your internal chaos and stand comfortably in your individuality with your recovering partner is one of the greatest challenges you'll face. You don't want to continue feeling so scared that you end up acting controlling over and over again. But if you do find yourself spying on your partner, or trying to control his or her every move, understand that you are being driven by fear; you aren't necessarily some sort of tyrant. Your recovering partner probably knows this, too.

TRY THIS: Find Your Own Self

You can establish boundaries by negotiating them with your partner or by taking actions without your partner. Imposing the following boundaries on yourself will help you break out of an enmeshed state:

- *Change the passwords on your e-mail account, cell phone, and computer and keep them private.*

- *Don't open mail addressed to your partner, even if you think it's junk mail.*

- *Observe yourself closely and see if you can catch when you are obsessing about your partner. Say to yourself, "Oops." Then turn your attention to something else. Anything else.*

- *For two whole days, do nothing for your partner that he or she can do for himself or herself.*

- *Don't call your partner's friends looking for him or her.*

- *Don't ask your partner a second time if he or she remembered to do something you asked him or her to do. Actively tolerate your frustration by breathing and saying to yourself, "Watching, watching, watching."*

- *Go to sleep earlier than your partner.*

- *Stay up later than your partner.*

- *If someone asks you how your partner is doing, say, "I'm not sure. But how are you?"*

- *One night a week, whether you feel like it or not, go out with a friend.*

These are a few of the things you can do to get a feel for being a separate person from your partner. Whether you try some of these suggestions or create your own, mindfully take note of what comes up for you and what you learn about yourself in the process.

TRY THIS: Keep a Journal

One way to better handle the thoughts and feelings and sensations that arise during the process of creating boundaries and beefing up your separate self is to write. Writing is an activity that involves the prefrontal cortex of your brain. Your neocortex, in particular, plays an important role in making appropriate responses to your environment. That includes reactions to your partner! On the other hand, the more primitive parts of your brain, known as the reptilian brain or limbic system, lack the sane reasoning power of your prefrontal cortex. Writing reengages your prefrontal cortex.

Write down in a journal all the various ways you are behaving as a separate person from your partner. Which behaviors have been easy for you? Which have been difficult? Describe what you are learning as a result of making these changes, how you feel, and what you hope will come of your efforts. Write every day for thirty days.

At the end of thirty days, buy yourself a gift for the good work you have done. Nothing that's going to break the bank, but something that is clearly a special reward. It always helps to reinforce yourself for doing things right, as opposed to only noticing when you are making mistakes. Of course, getting to a new level of independence in your relationship and feeling more at home in your own company will be the best gift of all.

Question: "Why Do I Need Treatment? My Partner's the One with the Problem."

When I met Susan, I would never have suspected from her trim and tidy appearance that she was slowly dying of emotional deprivation in her marriage. She told me she met her husband, Alessandro, in Italy when she was sixteen. She convinced him to come to America, and they got married shortly after she turned eighteen. She still felt guilty, even after all these years, about taking her husband away from his homeland. Susan said, "I made my bed, so I guess I have to lie in it."

I asked, "What exactly are you saying you're lying in?"

Susan mentioned that she had been suffering from anxiety attacks and insomnia for a year, but her bigger concern was her husband's excessive gambling and drinking. She admitted to being so entrenched in the relationship that it was impossible to consider separation. She said, "I can't live with him and I can't leave him. I can't abandon him. He gave up his life in Italy to be with me. Don't I owe him the same in return?"

I said, "I understand. You're just trying to be a loving person."

She said, "Exactly."

Like most people who struggle with codependency, Susan thought love meant having no boundaries, loyalty meant self-sacrifice, and being understanding meant making excuses for addictive behavior. Her mood swings and anxiety were classic examples of someone with both feet in an addict partner's shoes.

I said, "If the description you've given me of Alessandro is accurate, it sounds like you're living with someone who is an addict." I asked her if she was interested in hearing about the kinds of treatment available for her husband or if she was just seeking help for herself.

She told me her husband had no interest in getting treatment and she had no interest in going to any kind of recovery program either. She gave me a response I've heard over and over again: "I don't understand. Why do I need treatment? He's the one with the problem."

I know better than to argue with anyone who follows this line of thinking. It is easy to keep focusing on the addict and the obviously out-of-control, progressively worse behavior that the disease drives your addicted partner toward. Why would you think you need treatment when you know that your real problem is being a victim of the addict? Yet it is this very attitude that makes it take longer to connect the dots between being a codependent and leaping into your own recovery.

Most people who suffer from codependency are scared to change their own actions, even if those actions aren't producing the results they are looking for. If you are in this position, rest assured that you don't have to do anything you don't want to do or don't feel ready to do. You can take as little or as much of the advice offered to you by others as you wish. However, try not to dismiss any advice too quickly. Although Susan had no interest in checking out a program for herself, I gave her the simple homework assignment I've given you—mindfully taking up a hobby. She chose to join a gym and also a book club to which one of her friends had invited her. This was a turning point. Her mood improved as she began to exercise regularly, though still not enough to feel great; so her doctor prescribed an antidepressant, which further helped her mood.

As a result of feeling better, Susan started showing signs not only of self-regard, but of a healthy anger toward her husband for the ways he was exploiting their marriage. Instead of feeling guilty, she was finally getting mad! I knew these feelings were lighting a fire under her to start setting boundaries she would never have considered before.

One Partner Gets into Recovery First

Let's consider the situation, such as that faced by Susan and Alessandro, in which one partner is still actively in addiction and the other is not. If that latter partner is you, you can start setting better boundaries, whether your partner is on board or not. However, you need to know what can happen if you make unilateral changes—that is, if you take action (such as reading this book, seeing a shrink, or going to a 12-step or any other self-help program) without your partner knowing about it or agreeing. Your partner may react in one of three ways.

First, your partner may notice that you are acting differently and say, "Hey, what are you up to? Why are you acting that way?" Often this is not a sign of friendly interest, but one of suspicion. Your partner may acknowledge your efforts, but that doesn't mean his or her behavior will change; in fact, it may get more defensive. In this case, you have made a change in the right direction, but your efforts alone haven't improved the relationship. For example, you start to ignore comments that would otherwise escalate into a fight, or you become less available during your free time. When your partner accuses you of being up to no good, you may feel frustrated in your efforts to change. At worst, you may feel bullied into abandoning your efforts. This is the time when staying steadfast really counts.

Second, your partner may be oblivious to the changes you're making. Strangely, you may start to feel better about your relationship anyway. In this case, the boundaries you establish change how you feel, and that affects choices you make about the relationship. For example, you start hanging out with your own friends a couple times a week and enjoy doing things with them that your partner is not interested in doing. You don't make a big deal about it and are casual when you mention your plans. You are happy with your changes, and your partner simply goes with the flow. This may help you feel less entangled with your partner and give you room to breathe more easily, but it doesn't mean you don't still have a list of things you'd like to see changed in your relationship.

Third, your partner may notice that you are being less involved, holding your own a little better, and being more loving, and in turn start to react to you in a similar way. You might even start to talk openly together about things that are bothering you or changes you would like to see in the relationship, or just begin sharing more about yourself because the atmosphere feels better between you. This last outcome is ideal. It shows that your efforts to set new boundaries and become a change agent have improved not only your own well-being, but the well-being of your relationship. Hallelujah!

MINDFULNESS MEDITATION:
Finding Your Boundaries Within

Remember, as we saw in chapter 1, you are the observer of your world. Even if your partner is still actively in addiction, you don't need to go along for the ride. You can simply observe your feelings. Use the following mindful meditation to notice when feelings that historically kept you glued to your partner arise.

Read these instructions to yourself, then put down the book and do the meditation.

1. Close your eyes. Take a deep breath in and a long, slow breath out, and allow yourself to relax. Notice where you are holding tension in your body. Breathe into those places and allow yourself to relax more fully.

2. Now allow your mind to explore the concept of boundaries. Notice what you feel as you explore the word "boundary." What thoughts come up? What sensations do you feel in your body? Give yourself the freedom to discover exactly where your boundaries are.

3. Visualize yourself in different contexts with your partner—for example, at a restaurant, in your bathroom, at a friend's

house, at the beach, in bed. In each case, see if you can sense whether you feel close to or distant from your partner. Notice what your partner does that makes you feel this way. Become fully aware of the fact that you have the right to be comfortable with your partner and the right to find your voice with everyone you know. Allow yourself as much time as you need to explore your boundaries and to appreciate your ever-evolving relationship with each and every one of them.

4. Whenever you feel ready, open your eyes. Continue to stay present with your experience as you read on.

Question: "How Much Am I Supposed to Help My Partner After He or She Has Gotten into Recovery?"

Week after agonizing week, Alessandro continued to gamble and drink excessively. I watched as Susan kept cleaning up the financial messes he continued to make. I listened to her complaints and tried to sympathize with her feelings of helplessness.

One day Susan came in crying and revealed that her husband had taken jewelry from her family inheritance and pawned it for gambling money. However, she still wasn't ready to make any big decisions. She ended by saying, "I don't feel strong enough to leave, and I'm too angry to stay. I need a burning bush to show me what to do." I heard her desperate plea and told her to go home and keep an eye out for the sign she so badly wanted.

A week later Susan came in looking like a weight had been lifted from her shoulders. She said, "It finally happened. I got my burning bush. Alessandro came home from work drunk last night. He walked in with a wet coat and thought it would be brilliant to dry it off in our oven. The damn thing caught on fire and nearly burned down the house. Suddenly the lights went on in my head! Here was my burning bush. Literally! I realized it was time to save myself, with or without him." In that moment, Susan finally crossed the line onto the playing field of first stage recovery from codependency.

With that, Susan started going to a therapy group for partners of addicts, joined a meditation group, opened a separate checking account, and told Alessandro that either he got some help or the marriage was over. She was finally ready to pack her bags, but instead her husband packed his and checked into a twenty-eight-day rehab.

While Alessandro was away, Susan began to wonder how she would deal with him when he came home. She came in with a question family members so often ask: "How much am I supposed to help my partner after he's gotten into recovery?"

Wanting to help your partner in ways you never should have in the first place won't necessarily stop just because he or she is now in recovery. In fact, the urge to have your life revolve around your partner can get even worse! I will tell you the same thing I told Susan: "You're officially fired from the job of helping your partner. You know why? Because it's your turn now. Time to take your eyes off of your partner's needs and start focusing on your own. Your partner's recovery from addiction is his or her problem, and your recovery from codependency is yours."

Nutty as it may sound, your partner often needs you to walk away and ignore how he or she is working his or her program of recovery. This is true even if your partner relapses and starts drinking, gambling, drugging, sexting, overeating, or pursuing some other addiction. Neither the recovery nor the relapse of your partner is under your control. You may feel you are being neglectful by being less involved, but you are actually being respectful. Need I say that again? Help is about respecting someone enough *not* to help him or her. It is about believing that the person you chose to be in partnership with is just as capable of standing on his or her own two feet as you are.

As difficult as it may feel to do, if you can stop helping your partner now that he or she has finally gotten into recovery, he or she is more likely to grow up and be able to take care of you when you need it and love you the way you want. Bottom line, it's really the only way you will ever discover how much love and responsible action your partner can bring to the table.

Whether or not your recovering partner is doing his or her part as a positive change agent, as long as you're doing your part, you can't lose. Your changes will strengthen you, with or without your partner on board. If you're going solo in your efforts, you will gain the clarity necessary to know if you're in the right relationship. Eventually your burning bush will arrive.

TRY THIS: The Mindful True/False Boundary Quiz

Now it's time to check how you're doing. I realize it takes practice, but perhaps you've made some progress in establishing and maintaining boundaries in your relationship. Obviously, if you've just spent the last fifteen minutes reading this chapter for the first time, we can't expect that you've already transformed. So you may want to come back to this exercise again after a few weeks.

Read the following statements. Answer each one by indicating whether it is true or false for you. It may be hard to come to a definitive conclusion for some of them, so just go through and respond based on your gut feeling. Be mindful as you do this exercise. Allow yourself to breathe deeply. There is no need to judge what is true or false. Most statements won't seem 100 percent true or false, so go with your predominant feeling. Think of this exercise as a fact-finding mission to discover where you are at this moment in time. It's okay if your answers change tomorrow, next week, or next month. But tomorrow isn't here, so let's stick with today.

You may want to ask your recovering partner to answer these questions himself or herself, as well. If he or she looks at you like you've really gone crazy this time, just say, "Okay, no problem. I'm having fun with this. Let me know if you change your mind!"

1. I feel fine if my partner hasn't checked in with me during the day. It's probably for good reason.

   TRUE   FALSE

2. I feel fine if my partner doesn't share all the details of his or her life with me. After all, I don't share every detail about myself.

   TRUE   FALSE

3. I feel perfectly comfortable if my partner makes plans to do things without me. In fact, it's nice because I need some downtime.

   TRUE   FALSE

4. I'm not offended if my partner doesn't feel like talking about something I want to talk about. We have plenty of other things to talk about.

   TRUE   FALSE

5. I'm glad my partner doesn't want unsolicited advice from me anymore. I have enough to think about taking care of my own life.

   TRUE   FALSE

6. I'm not threatened that my partner now turns to other people for advice. I have plenty of friends I turn to, as well.

   TRUE   FALSE

7. I'm proud my partner has started a new hobby that doesn't include me. It actually makes things more interesting around here!

TRUE   FALSE

8. I'm relieved my partner is no longer looking to me for approval. I don't want to be a parent—I want to be a partner!

TRUE   FALSE

9. I'm relieved my partner is reacting less to me. I didn't like having so much power over him or her when we got into recovery.

TRUE   FALSE

10. I'm finally caring more about my own well-being and less about my partner's. That doesn't mean I love him or her any less.

TRUE   FALSE

If you answered true to all ten statements, your sense of your own autonomy is strong and you have the right attitude toward your partner, as well. If you haven't already tried to set and maintain boundaries, doing so will be fairly effortless for you.

If you answered true to six to nine statements, you are well on your way to getting the kind of strength you need to be a separate, yet interdependent, partner. Keep going. You're on the right track.

If you answered true to three to five statements, you are alternating between enmeshment and glimpses of self-empowerment. You need to keep making your boundaries clearer and letting your partner do the same. You are on the playing field of second stage recovery, but have a little more work to do to feel solid.

If you answered true to only one or two statements, you are not getting enough support. You need more advice from good friends, teachers, shrinks, or other people who are experts on relationships.

If you didn't answer true to any of the statements, then you are floating in a world where you aren't reaching out for help and are still glued to your partner. This is good to know, because now you can consciously consider whether you want to stay glued or get unglued. Remember: there is plenty of help available, and now is the time for you to ask for it!

Conclusion

You make hundreds of moves all day, every day, that could potentially push the boundaries of your relationship. I'm not suggesting you start feeling all precious like the princess and the pea and micromanage your relationship with hundreds of boundaries. That would make life too tense and rigid. I am suggesting you allow yourself to become more aware of where your partner ends and you begin, and how you bump up against each other or merge.

Obviously, if your partner is not on board with recovery—as was the case with Susan and Alessandro—most of the boundaries you set won't be negotiated. In the best of all worlds, however, you will have back-and-forth conversations about boundaries. I recognize this may sound scary if you have never done it before. You may have had little or no practice negotiating anything with your recovering partner, let alone something as tricky as personal boundaries. Moving from enmeshment to interdependence does not happen overnight. But creating and maintaining boundaries will get easier over time. As with anything, the more you do it, the better you will get at it.

Learning to be separate yet connected to your recovering partner will help you not just tolerate your differences, but also actually enjoy them. If you haven't experienced this yet, you have something special to look forward to. What used to be fine when you were an enmeshed couple—sharing straws and passwords, finishing your partner's sentences—will no longer be what you're fighting for once you've gotten a taste of freedom from enmeshment. In fact, you'll know instinctively that you're barking up the wrong tree when you ignore your boundaries and slide back into codependency. Regardless of where you are right now, congratulations on embarking on the real work of mindfully taking your feet out of your partner's shoes and putting them in your own.

CHAPTER 4

Moods and Emotions: Living with the Ups and Downs

How many times has the following scenario happened to you? You're in a perfectly good mood. Your day has had the usual mix of pleasure and aggravation, but you're still walking with your head held high. You have completed frustrating tasks and navigated your way around the personality quirks of your coworkers. You drive home singing along to your favorite tunes on the radio.

Then you get home. And your recovering partner gets home. You greet each other. You start a conversation. A minute later, your partner either looks at you funny or says the wrong thing. Now, for the life of you, you can't drop it. Even after he or she apologizes for hurting your feelings, you can't let it go. Unfortunately, sometimes being in a relationship with someone in recovery can make you feel as lonely or as upset as you were when he or she was buried in addiction.

There's no getting around it: the moods and emotions you and your partner have will feel more glaring and more obtrusive now that he or she is in recovery. You may hurt each other or lose your connection by insensitively expressing anger, frustration, or irritation. Or you may neglect each other due to mismanaged depression, estrangement, or self-pity. Rest assured, this is quite normal. It may not always be fun, but it is normal. It is wonderful that your partner is in recovery from addiction, but now is the time to prepare to face chaotic moods and erratic emotions.

In addition to the influence of your historical frame of reference and the continued lure of enmeshment, you may now feel emotionally naked in the face of the sadness, hurt, trauma, and anger that were swept under the rug while you tended to your partner's addiction. Rearing their ugly heads, these feelings demand your attention and refuse to be ignored. And guess what? This is true for your recovering partner as well!

Both partners are invariably convinced that they are the easier person to live with, even if they admit that their emotionality or insensitivity can "sometimes" be a challenge. It is the oldest form of delusion in the book, and it cuts across all codependents and all recovering addicts. I sit with couples from all walks of life daily, and inevitably each partner will look at me with pleading eyes, as if to say, "Can you believe what I have to put up with?" Then comes the eye-rolling disdain. They might as well be wearing one of those T-shirts that say, "I'm with stupid," with the arrow pointing right at their partner sitting next to them.

Your partner's addiction has been arrested, and yet you may feel trapped like a rat in a cage. This chapter will show you how to manage your moods and emotions more effectively by understanding how your brain functions and by making the right lifestyle changes, so that you can breathe more easily and feel more empowered in your relationship.

Moods and Emotions

Let's look more closely at the nature of mood and emotion. Although the terms often are used interchangeably, there is a subtle difference between them. A *mood* is an internal state of subjectivity that feels either good or bad. Good and bad moods can distort our perception of the outside world, thus affecting how we relate to others. For example, you wake up in a bad mood and see the world through a negative lens. Your partner can do no right, and you feel out of sorts with yourself, as well. Or you wake up in a good mood and find yourself whistling through your day, giving your partner the benefit of the doubt regardless of whatever missteps he or she may make.

We all feel at the mercy of our moods from time to time. But when a person is in a bad mood for too long, or swings from extreme highs to extreme lows, we call that a *mood disorder*. People with mood disorders (for example, depression, bipolar disorder, anxiety or panic disorders) suffer with extreme bad moods for days, weeks, or months at a time if they don't seek outside help. Mood disorders are very disruptive to your well-being and to your ability to connect with others.

Emotions, in contrast, are activated more specifically in response to something in our world that provokes us. For example, when someone cuts you off in traffic, you get a parking ticket, or a check you wrote bounces, you feel a flash of anger, which you may or may not express in that moment. Emotions typically don't last as long as moods. They come and go and can change quickly, depending on what is stimulating them. However, they can lurk under the surface, especially if not expressed. In the case of the parking ticket, for example, when you get home hours later, you may suddenly find yourself yelling at your partner in anger. You may have forgotten about the ticket, but your anger has been waiting for a chance to express itself. Sometimes emotions that we don't express or that go unresolved can eventually manifest as moods. Unlike moods, however, once an emotion has been ignited, we can usually pinpoint its source. Because emotions are more specific than moods, it can also be easier to express them.

Breaking the Autopilot Habit

I'm sure there have been times you scarcely noticed where you were emotionally all day. Conversely, you may have gone through the day so consumed with bad moods and emotions you couldn't think of much else. Both are ways of being on autopilot. Either way, there's nothing like a little recovery coming into your life to make you sit up and take notice.

TRY THIS: Mindfully Take Your Emotional Pulse

Mindfully breaking the habit of being on autopilot is pretty easy once you get the hang of it. This simple exercise will teach you how to mindfully check in with yourself about how you're feeling. I'm not promoting the habit of navel gazing, but I am asking you to step out of your routine, pause, and look inward. Remember to let whatever's there register without judgment.

1. Ask yourself: "What exactly am I feeling right at this moment? Am I feeling happy? Sad? Mad? Afraid? Numb? Disjointed? Flooded? On automatic pilot?" Your feelings can be pleasant or unpleasant, rational or irrational.

2. Just let your feelings do their thing. Notice them the way you would watch fish swimming in an aquarium. Let your feelings swim around like little fish, and take note of their colors,

sensations, and movements. Identify and watch them as they float by. You can't control your feelings, but you can control your relationship to them by using mindful awareness.

If you do this exercise three times a day for thirty days, you will start to build a buffer, or pause, between how you're feeling and thinking and how you end up acting. This practice of checking in with yourself will give you the power to control your actions rather than letting them control you.

TRY THIS: Mindfully Unhinge Your Mind from Bad Feelings

This is a walking mindful meditation that is useful if you have the tendency to get pulled down by extremely bad feelings, moods, or mental states that drown you in fear and agitation.

1. Take a walk for a minimum of thirty minutes. Use this time as an opportunity to redirect your attention from your moods and emotions toward the environment around you.

2. With every step you take, notice the sounds, the smells, and the sights. Experience the colors you see. Feel the air around you as you breathe. Notice how your feet feel as they take each step.

3. As you do this, say to yourself, "Walking, walking, walking," over and over again. If you prefer, you can say, "Watching, watching, watching." The effect is the same.

4. If you are feeling especially agitated or depressed, try speeding your walk up to a more brisk pace. As your mood settles, return to a slower walking pace.

Question: "Why Is My Partner Distant and in a Bad Mood All the Time Now That He or She Is in Recovery?"

Most people overestimate their positive impact on their partners and underestimate the negative. For example, you might think that glaring with hostility at your partner for a moment is no big deal. But that brief glare can fuel a power struggle and create or intensify bad blood or feelings of alienation. Mishandling a bad mood leaves both of you lonely, wandering around in an icy atmosphere.

Take the case of Sally and Ben, who had been together for seven years and had two young children. Ben had been in recovery for one year from compulsive online gambling for money and gaming for amusement.

During our initial session, Sally said flat out, "I'm at the end of my rope and ready to call it quits. I've been bending over backwards to make Ben happy, but he wouldn't be happy even if he were in paradise. He rarely wants to spend time with the children or me, and continues to isolate himself for hours on end. I'm glad that he's off that damn computer, but honestly, things don't feel that much better."

Ben glared at Sally and retorted, "Ever since I've gotten into recovery, I've felt rotten. Sally keeps accusing me of having no interest in her, but I'm really tired and anxious and have very little sex drive. On weekends, I take a nap during the day, but I still feel exhausted. Between the way I feel and having to deal with Sally's chronic nagging, it's a wonder I haven't run back to the computer again."

Sally and Ben were at war with each other because neither could make sense of the feelings they were having. Worse yet, the more Sally reached out to Ben for clarity, or connection, or a little comforting, the more he pulled away. And the more he pulled away, the more forcefully she came after him. By the time I met them, this dynamic had been well-worn into their relationship.

In Sally's mind, once Ben woke up to the fact that he was an addict and got off the computer, he should have been eager to make things up to his family. She had heard from a friend that the addict's job was to make amends to everyone for all the ways he or she had caused harm while in addiction. That wasn't happening.

"Whenever I try to engage Ben, he treats me as if I'm asking for the world," she said. "I just don't get it. Why is he so distant and in such a bad mood all the time now that he is in recovery?"

I'm not going to get too scientific on you, but you might be better able to handle negative moods and emotions with a little more understanding about the biology of the brain.

Our brain releases many chemicals, called *neurotransmitters*, which play a big role in determining how we feel. For example, serotonin is a neurotransmitter that makes us feel happy. Simply put, when the synaptic connection goes haywire and the brain is deprived of serotonin saturation, we tend to feel anxious, apathetic, depressed, fatigued, or irritated. Another neurotransmitter, called dopamine, affects how we experience pleasure or pain. Finally, a third neurotransmitter called norepinephrine affects focus and enhances mood. We have many neurotransmitters in our brain, but these three are the biggies that, when in balance, spark the electrical activity that keeps us feeling happy, alert, and focused. When we are under too much stress, these same neurotransmitters can stop firing properly, causing us to feel out of balance.

What might drive a person to feel distant? Angry all the time? Numb? You might think I'm secretly trying to get you to a shrink so that you can delve into the cause of all your feelings, but that's not where I'm going with this. It is important to recognize that difficulties with moods and emotions don't derive solely from your historical frame of reference; they are also a result of your neurobiology, physiology, and lifestyle. In other words, this is where you stop blaming the way your parents raised you and start blaming your DNA.

Moods and emotions are felt in what we consider to be our heart, but it's our brain that drives them. The memories we hold, our mentality, and how our neurons fire in our brain all determine how moods and emotions are served up to us. You might also find it useful to learn the basics of how the brain of an addict works.

The Addict's Brain

When an addict engages in his or her addiction of choice, the brain releases vast amounts of dopamine, serotonin, and norepinephrine, creating sensations of euphoria. It doesn't matter whether the addiction is to cocaine or to gambling—a similar release of chemicals occurs in the brain, triggering the addict to repeat that choice over and over again in order to continue getting a rush of good feeling.

Each addiction disrupts neurotransmitters in particular ways, but all evoke initial pleasurable feelings, followed by subsequent dependence. One might think that arresting harmful addiction would automatically bring back a natural balance to the neurotransmitters of the brain. Ideally, this would be the case. But it rarely is. Instead, addiction so profoundly befuddles the activity of neurotransmitters—either by overexciting the transfer of messages within the brain, or by interfering with those messages—that to help the addict's brain function properly again can require great care, time, and professional attention.

By the time an addict finally stops his or her behavior, his or her neurotransmitters are pooped out, leaving the newly recovering addict with symptoms of depression, anxiety, intense cravings, extreme fatigue, angry outbursts, lack of motivation, and irritability. The neurotransmitters that flooded the addict with good feelings are no longer present, and bad moods and negative feelings take their place. Even if the addict knows that his or her addictive behavior is self-destructive, he or she may be unable to resist engaging in it. The anticipated relief associated with that behavior is simply too powerful. It's no wonder addicts end up feeling like their moods and feelings are an enemy. The addict's inability to handle his or her negative emotions in recovery is one of the major reasons for relapse.

Dry Syndrome

Traditionally, "dry drunk" refers to the alcoholic who has stopped drinking but hasn't made any lifestyle changes and who continues to act in the same ways as when he or she was drinking. We now know the same syndrome can express itself in anyone who abstains from any addiction. For this reason, I prefer to call it simply *dry syndrome*. If this is happening to your partner, you can expect his or her moods to be awful. Your partner will be miserable and overly reactive and, well, just not a happy camper.

Similarly, what I call *dry codependent syndrome* occurs when codependents continue to act and live in the same way they did before their partner got into recovery. They are still watching their recovering partner's life, rather than working on their own. They stay irritated and anxious. Let's take a closer look at how dry codependent syndrome expresses itself, and what you can do to get out of it.

TRY THIS: Are You Experiencing Dry Codependent Syndrome?

To determine if you are suffering from dry codependent syndrome, read the following statements and check all that apply.

☐ *You experience abrupt shifts from depression to anxious agitation.*

☐ *You lack the ability to express your feelings and emotions openly without causing alienation in the partnership.*

☐ *You feel no gratitude for your life.*

☐ You feel bitter and pessimistic.

☐ You don't care anymore whether your partner stays on a recovering track.

☐ You feel alienated and alone in the world.

☐ You lack a practice of introspection, contemplative solitude, or service to others.

☐ You actively avoid emotional connection or attachment with friends.

☐ You struggle with extreme moodiness and agitation.

☐ You feel seething resentment toward your partner, regardless of how nice he or she is toward you.

☐ You feel easily infuriated toward your partner.

☐ You want to isolate yourself for long periods of time, rather than connect with your partner.

☐ You feel chaotic, erratic, and scared much of the time.

☐ You feel out of touch with the purpose of your life.

☐ Everything and everyone seems stupid and insensitive.

☐ You feel lonely, even when you're with friends.

☐ Nothing is enough to fill the hole in your gut.

☐ Wherever you are, you wish you were somewhere else.

☐ You feel burdened by having to reach out to others.

☐ You feel obsessed with how your partner is working his or her program of recovery, and you can't give him or her some needed space.

If you identify with five or more of these statements, you can consider yourself to be experiencing dry codependent syndrome.

The misery a dry state creates isn't the kind of normal suffering with which one has to live. It's not the kind you sit and meditate on; it's the kind where you get up off your chair and go out to get the right kind of support.

Rule Out Any Underlying Causes

Unlike a stunned couple in first stage recovery, still rowing around in a sea of denial, Ben and Sally were grappling with dry syndrome in second stage recovery. I knew they needed the right interventions to help them develop a steady mood. The first was for Ben to rule out any underlying medical conditions that could be the primary reason for his persistent bad mood. Ben agreed to schedule an appointment with his regular doctor for a checkup.

TRY THIS: Self-Checkup

Before you schedule your own visit to your doctor, perform this mini-checkup on yourself. Read through the following list and put a check mark next to any items that pertain to you:

- ☐ I drink three or more cups of coffee every day of the week.

- ☐ I eat foods high in refined sugar regularly.

- ☐ My family has a history of depression.

- ☐ My family has a history of mental illness.

- ☐ My family has a history of alcoholism or other addiction.

- ☐ My family has a history of anxiety disorders.

- ☐ I have never had my thyroid checked.

- ☐ I have taken myself off one or more of my prescribed medications without consulting my doctor.

☐ I am going through menopause.

☐ I suffer from depression.

☐ I suffer from anxiety.

☐ I suffer from a mental illness.

☐ I take steroids for inflammation.

☐ I have arthritis and can't exercise.

☐ I don't sleep well.

☐ I take medication for asthma.

☐ I take decongestants for allergies.

☐ I smoke cigarettes.

☐ I have a history of the Epstein-Barr virus (also known as chronic fatigue syndrome).

☐ I have high blood pressure.

☐ I don't exercise.

☐ I drink less than three cups of water a day.

It you checked three or more items on this list and your moods are hard to control, it is time for a checkup with your doctor. Your doctor may recommend some specific changes of lifestyle, diet, or medication to help you get better control of your moods.

Tending Your Garden

Picture your relationship as a garden that started in full bloom. When your bad moods led you to treat your partner with hostility, disdain, criticalness, or neglect, the soil in your garden became poisoned, and your flowers and plants eventually died. No one, of course, strives to end up with just weeds and rocks in the garden of his or her relationship. Learning different ways to soothe your negative moods will help keep your garden in full bloom. How have you been tending your garden?

Your relationship depends on your gaining mastery over your bad moods and negative emotions. Without that, you will be at the mercy of the only things that grow in contaminated relationship soil: relapse and ugly fighting, as well as unfortunate separations and breakups. Ultimately, it's your soil, and it's up to you to till it, fertilize it, and maintain it.

Medicine to Manage Moods

Living with a recovering partner who is spending his or her days in misery from uncontrolled moodiness and emotional reactivity won't teach either of you anything worth learning; it will only keep bringing you and your relationship down. If a serious mood disorder is left untreated, your partner will be on a slippery slope, and ultimately your survival as a couple may be threatened. So if your recovering partner's doctor suggests that he or she take a medication, by all means, support this course of action! Your partner deserves a fighting chance to be well and to have his or her moods regulated by the right medication when necessary.

The right medicines can improve your partner's chances of staying addiction-free long term and keeping his or her mood buoyant throughout the day. This does not give you license to start prodding your partner to go get medication, though. Remember: you don't have control over what your recovering partner does or does not do to make his or her life more comfortable. It just helps to recognize that mood disorders can coexist with addiction during recovery.

Sally supported Ben when his doctor determined he was suffering from a mood disorder known as agitated depression, and prescribed an antidepressant. He began to feel relief within a few weeks. His mood became more cheerful, he was able to be more open, and he started behaving more generously toward Sally. He talked with her more, showed more interest in their kids, and even organized a family vacation.

Question: "Why Am I Still So Anxious Now That My Recovering Partner Has Been Treated for Depression and His or Her Mood Is So Much Better?"

Sally noticed Ben getting more involved and closer to her, yet she felt no less anxious. In fact, her anxiety seemed to get worse. For example, when Ben planned the vacation—something she used to complain he never did—she found herself coming up with irrational reasons why it was a bad idea to go. She expressed fear that Ben would revert to his gambling habit if he had too much free time on his hands at the resort. And when Ben made overt romantic advances, she got angry and pushed him away.

Sally didn't understand what was happening. She asked, "Why am I still so anxious now that Ben has been treated for depression and his mood is so much better?"

It is very common for a codependent's suppressed feelings and mood issues to express themselves at the same time that his or her recovering partner is getting into better shape. The well of anxiety, anger, resentment, and hurt that had been eclipsed by Sally's revolving around Ben's addiction, and then around his agitated depression in recovery, suddenly had space to reveal itself. The result of Ben's addressing his mood disorder and making positive behavioral changes was a mixed bag for Sally. On the one hand, she was relieved he was doing something constructive to deal with his agitated depression.

On the other hand, Ben's changes were forcing her to attend to the feelings and pain that previously had been masked.

I've never met a codependent who consciously opted to continue suffering in a state of fear and anxiety when his or her recovering partner was seeking connection. But even with the best of intentions, a recovering addict can't erase the havoc his or her addiction caused in the relationship overnight. In the short term, seeing Ben's new and improved mood was not enough to heal the wounds Sally had incurred from a long history of disconnection, alienation, and isolation. While he was active in his addictions, he had behaved in ways that betrayed Sally emotionally. Understandably, she remained anxious even after he got into recovery, because she unconsciously anticipated further betrayal at any moment.

Post-Traumatic Stress Disorder

Sally said, "Ben's mood seems much better. It isn't perfect, but we've been getting along and spending quality time together. However, I'm not used to having him close and being able to trust him. I'm afraid to let my guard down because some of the ways he's still acting are triggering terrible reactions in me."

What Sally was expressing is known as post-traumatic stress disorder (PTSD). Emotional pain has many ways of expressing itself. It can come out fighting, or it can go underground and hide in the crevices of our brain. Pain that we store in our brain is usually associated with trauma. When you think of trauma, you may associate it first and foremost with war, child abuse, violence, sexual abuse, natural disasters, or tragic accidents. But trauma can also be caused by the unpredictable nature of addiction.

Even though Ben had gotten control over the threatening behavior he exhibited while active in his addiction, at times Sally continued to react to him with panic attacks and uncontrollable tears, as she had when he was still gambling. For example, if he stayed in his room alone for too long, seemed too distant, or became frustrated easily with the kids, she had extreme reactions that made her ready to intervene with severe measures that seemed out of proportion to what Ben was actually doing. This confused both Sally and Ben.

When PTSD goes unrecognized, it can cause or contribute to a codependent person's anxiety, and provoke exaggerated responses of hypervigilance, outbursts of anger, sleep disturbances, high blood pressure, backaches, stomachaches, migraines, depression, and agitated moods. These emotional and physical symptoms are also associated with many other disorders, but in the case of PTSD, they are triggered by painful *implicit memories*: that is, memories that you act out of automatically, rather than ones you consciously recall. Implicit memories are stored in the amygdala (which is part of the limbic system), and include both traumatic and nontraumatic experiences.

When traumatic implicit memories are ignited, you don't feel as if they are coming from the past; you feel as if they are happening in the present. For example, suppose your partner always came home late at night when he or she was active in addiction. Now when it starts to get late and your recovering partner isn't home, you feel a stomachache, anxiety, or nausea, even though rationally you know there is nothing to worry about. In spite of what you tell yourself, triggers arise from situations that mimic the past and cause your symptoms to flare up. Untreated trauma from the past becomes the lens through which you view the present and predict the future.

Like Sally, you may feel baffled and frustrated that a subtle sense of threat still lurks within your recovering relationship. Even after you've talked over the same material again and again, the lines of security remain thin. If you are experiencing this, you may be suffering from PTSD. It is important to recognize and treat PTSD because it can not only cause strife within a relationship, but also lead you, the codependent, to fall back into old behaviors with your recovering partner. It is especially heartbreaking when a codependent becomes overwhelmed with PTSD and as a result chooses to separate from his or her recovering partner prematurely, without first attempting to address PTSD reactions. Don't make this mistake!

TRY THIS: Identify PTSD Reactions

Read the following statements and check off the ones that apply to you.

☐ I become overly anxious when my recovering partner leaves the house at night, even when I know where he or she is going.

☐ If my partner seems distant, I suddenly feel scared and even nauseated.

☐ I become agitated quickly if my recovering partner stays up too late at night.

☐ My heart starts to beat quickly if my recovering partner doesn't show up on time.

☐ If I wake up at night and my recovering partner is in the next room, my mind starts racing.

☐ Whenever my recovering partner gets into certain moods, I become frightened and can't think rationally.

☐ I get a sick feeling in my stomach when my recovering partner doesn't look me in the eye when I ask him or her a question.

☐ I can start to panic just watching television shows that portray addicts or alcoholics.

☐ I feel as if I'm leaving my body if my recovering partner gets angry with me.

☐ If a credit card company, bank, or other business phones, I feel I'm going to be sick without even knowing the nature of the call.

☐ If my recovering partner goes out of town on business, I am in a constant state of worry until he or she gets home.

☐ My back starts to hurt when I don't know where my recovering partner is.

☐ I get an immediate headache when my recovering partner's mood looks too happy.

☐ Certain sounds, such as the clicking of the key in a lock, can make me feel scared for no reason.

☐ Not a day goes by that I don't check the clock at specific times and wonder where my recovering partner is.

If you checked off five or more items, you may be struggling with PTSD.

Treating PTSD

PTSD doesn't have to be a scary diagnosis. Know that it will get better with patience and compassion from your partner and—if it persists—the help of a good therapist, as well. Finding a good therapist who knows how to heal trauma is invaluable. PTSD doesn't have to be a big, bad, scary diagnosis. Know that it will get better with patience and compassion from your partner and—if it persists—the help of a good therapist, as well. Finding a good therapist who knows how to heal trauma is invaluable. A number of PTSD treatments have been researched and shown to be quite effective. A list of these provided by Tori DeAngelis includes prolonged-exposure therapy, cognitive-processing therapy, and eye-movement desensitization and reprocessing (EMDR). EMDR, which was originally created by Francine Shapiro, uses movement of the eyes as a technique to clear out trauma held in the brain's implicit memory bank. Thus, it is a somatic therapy, meaning it involves the body, not just the mind. EMDR can address the kind of trauma that was caused by living with your partner's behavior during active addiction and is still disruptive to your everyday life.

In addition to seeking therapy, you can enlist the help of your recovering partner, if he or she is willing. I suggested that when Sally got into a state of mistrust, she allow Ben to soothe her. For example, he could simply look her in the eye and say gently, "I can totally understand how you would feel nervous or suspicious, but the last thing in the world I want to do is betray or hurt you. I'm as devoted to my recovery as you are, if not more." Sally responded well to this, and Ben felt relieved to have found words that were right for Sally and that gave him an opportunity to make up for lost time.

If your partner is not available to offer you sympathy, reassurance, or soothing, then you are going to have to find other ways to calm the anxiety from your PTSD. Obviously, in the best of all worlds, your partner would jump at the chance to be of service to your healing process, but now may not be the time for that.

TRY THIS: Mindfully Get to Know Your Inner Philosopher

As you get more in touch with your emotional pulse, you can start to mindfully investigate your inner world more deeply and help yourself get out from underneath the power of PTSD. Perhaps you're one of those people who, instead of being on autopilot, are hyperaware of your feelings. If so, you're probably motivated to get relief from the tyranny of stimulation overload to your nervous system.

As you learned in chapter 2, the act of writing is useful for bringing clarity of mind as well as emotional relief to the person doing the writing. That means you. Inviting the philosopher within you to mindfully write about how he or she thinks and feels is a way to give voice to that part of yourself and a great act of self-healing.

Take a pen and paper, or pull out your keyboard, and write down your answers to the following questions. I suggest you choose one question per day and focus on that. You don't have to answer them in any particular order.

What feelings am I still holding against my partner?

In what ways am I acting moody with my partner?

What reactions do I have now that I know are old reactions from when my partner was active in addiction?

What experiences from before my partner got into recovery have left me feeling traumatized?

What ways does my partner behave that contribute to my bad moods or negative feelings?

How would I tell the story of my own healing journey?

How am I willing to take complete responsibility for my physical, emotional, and mental health?

How would I like to express my moods and emotions in the future?

How have my moods and emotions affected my life in ways that have nothing to do with my partner?

How could taking time each day to disconnect from the stimulation of the world around me help me feel happier?

This is another exercise that is impossible to fail at. So don't even think about writer's block. I'm not asking you to write the next great American novel. Whatever you write will help put you in touch with the answers that already lie within you. And remember to mindfully take note of the feelings, sensations, and thoughts that arise.

If Your PTSD Antenna Remains Up

Although it is extremely reassuring to know your recovering partner is following a clear-cut path and you are getting the support you need, your PTSD antenna may still go up at the smallest signs of potential betrayal by your partner. Don't be impatient with yourself if it takes a while to break the habit of holding your breath, waiting for your partner's moods, emotions, and behavior to change so that you can relax and feel safe. You may have been working so hard to control the temperature of your partner's moods or how your partner chooses to work his or her program that you become stymied when he or she actually starts to do what makes you happy. You're still suspicious. You may have to talk to yourself a lot, breathe a lot, and reassure yourself over and over again that you really can stop anxiously hopping around and using up good energy trying to prevent bad things from happening.

TRY THIS: Bring Yourself Back to the Present Moment with Mindful Self-Talk

You can't stop your partner from relapsing or from having bad moods and reactive feelings, but you sure as heck can keep yourself steady, regardless. If your partner isn't willing to help soothe you or reassure you, have no fear. You can choose how to respond to your partner's moods moment by moment, day by day, and move toward empowering yourself in your relationship. For starters, let's investigate how your mind works when you are feeling afraid or anxious.

Self-talk is just what it sounds like. It is you talking to yourself, just not out loud. If you stop to think about it, you already talk to yourself all day long. The goal is to have your brain talk to you in the way you want it to, not in the automatic way it usually does. Unless, of course, you already know how to interrupt negative feelings with the right kind of self-talk that soothes your anxieties and returns you

113

to a state of faith and confidence. We don't want to tamper with that. If that is you, then this exercise is one you can skip.

The next time you're feeling anxious or fearful, here's what I suggest you do and say to yourself.

First, look around and mindfully take in the present. Be aware of your breath, and breathe deeply until you've calmed down a bit. Tell yourself, "Fear is having its way with me right now." Take a moment to consider this idea. It is hard to get control of your feelings if you can't stop long enough to notice what is actually happening within you.

Then speak to your fear from a position of strength. Say, "Fear, you have no power here! I'm the one in charge."

Tell yourself, "I'm going to resist the need to figure things out. I'm going to get off the fix-it trail. I'm going to sit back and relax. I am now letting go of control."

Now say to yourself, "Fear, begone!" And mean it. You must remind your brain that it has absolutely no control over whether your partner is up to no good or is going to relapse.

If you forget and revert to a fearful or anxious state, come back to this exercise. It isn't easy, but you can train your mind to stop spooking you into a state of terror. Specifically, you are using your mind to interrupt your irrational fears. It's the same thing you do when you turn to your partner or a close friend and allow him or her to reassure you that everything is going to be okay, and that you don't need to fearfully anticipate bad things. Only in this case, you're turning to yourself for some emotional nourishment.

How to Mindfully Soothe Anxiety Without Saying a Word

Soothing your own anxiety is a necessary ability, but so is being able to soothe each other when you're in a relationship. This next exercise only requires your willingness to sit still with your partner.

You don't have to be debonair, suave, or full of charisma to make a difference here. Just have the same excitement, curiosity, and anticipation that you might bring to a first date. After all, it's never too late to start having first dates with your partner again. This was the first exercise I had Ben and Sally do. The idea was to help Sally feel less anxious and to bring them closer now that Ben's mood was more stable and Sally's PTSD had been exposed.

TRY THIS: The Mindful Shoulder-to-Shoulder Connection

There are a variety of ways that you can mend your anxious, wobbly attachment to your partner and increase your intimacy and connection. Some you can do alone, and others involve your partner's help. This next exercise requires participation on the part of your partner. Again, if this is not possible right now, skip it and keep moving forward with the exercises you can do alone.

If your partner is game to do this exercise with you, together you can calm your nervous systems and create a bond, without either of you needing to speak one word. Couples in recovery already talk too much, focusing more in their heads than in their hearts. This exercise will bring you both back to your core. It's nice to count on a few minutes of gentle intimacy each day with each other, right?

Daily shoulder-to-shoulder sitting can turn things around in a subtle but steady way. Because this exercise creates greater safety between you, you will find it easier to soothe each other when feelings of anger, sadness, fear, or anxiety arise throughout your day. Regulating reactivity is of utmost importance in creating safety, especially when historical trauma has disrupted trust.

You can do this exercise sitting next to your partner on a sofa, in two chairs, or side by side on the floor. The only equipment you need is a timer, which you should set for three minutes.

When you are both seated comfortably, with your shoulders touching, direct your gaze toward the floor in front of you, or close your eyes. See if you can synchronize your breath with your partner's. Follow your breath and take notice of the sounds around you and the thoughts that go through your mind. Don't try to control anything.

There is no wrong way of doing this exercise. As long as you keep your butt on the seat and your shoulder next to your partner's for three minutes, you have succeeded. If you do this every day for thirty days you should feel calmer, safer, and less reactive with your partner.

Over time, as you practice this shoulder-to-shoulder exercise, it will become one of the ways to create feelings of comfort and security between you. Many people attest to learning a great deal from containing their reactivity and just sitting still. Not that you're in a race, but sitting still when you feel bad and not acting on those feelings can make all the difference between your partnership being held back in first stage recovery and moving on to second stage recovery.

Lifestyle No-Brainers

As we've already seen, just abstaining from addiction and codependent behavior is not enough to steer you toward positive moods and feelings. Apart from medical conditions, mood disorders, or PTSD, your lifestyle may become the most important key to your happiness and protection from living in a dry codependent state.

What I'm about to tell you is not anything you don't already know. It is Basic Life Advice 101. It is what I think of as a no-brainer. If your mother didn't harp on this, then surely one of your schoolteachers did, or a health-nut friend, or maybe even someone standing next to you at the checkout stand in the market.

Here it is: You *must* include healthy food, water, and exercise as part of your lifestyle if you want to feel really good and be free of old, codependent behaviors. Just as you had to get codependency out of your lifestyle, you now have to get healthy habits put in their place.

TRY THIS: Increasing Your Endorphins with Mindful Exercise

Mindful exercise is one of the most significant components of your new lifestyle. It is also a great way to enhance the bond between you and your recovering partner—and you don't even have to talk to each other to do it! This is because when we exercise, our brains release endorphins. Endorphins not only act as a natural painkiller, they also lower anxiety and enhance mood. Maybe you've heard of the so-called runner's high. I'm not advocating that you start doing something that's all about getting high; this phenomenon is backed by solid research. In 2008, Henning Boecker and his colleagues in Germany used a brain scanner to measure opioid levels in athletes' brains, and found an increase in endorphins after they had jogged for two hours. You don't need to go for quite that long, but put on your walking shoes and walk briskly with your partner for at least thirty minutes and until you break a sweat. Do this at least three times a week. Yes, you can bring the dog, too.

If walking isn't your thing, choose a type of exercise you like. Just make sure it is sufficiently active to trigger those endorphins. Whatever your preferred form of exercise, invite your recovering partner to join you in the activity. When you exercise together, both of you will experience an improvement in your mood almost immediately. Whether you are in first or second stage recovery, exercising side by side will increase the goodwill you feel toward each other.

Learn to Go with the Imperfect Flow of Relationship

As a codependent, knowing when to soothe yourself and when to turn to your partner for comfort is easier said than done. It can be tricky when you're working hard to find a balance between attending to your own moods and emotions and trying to stay connected to your recovering partner without getting overly entangled. Becoming more mindful of yourself is a lifelong practice.

I can't show you how to achieve a perfect relationship in which you will never have any bad moods, and you and your recovering partner will never act badly toward each other again. That would be a book about living alone in a cave or a mountain top somewhere—*alone* being the operative word. If you want enduring human companionship, then the best strategy is to learn how to flow with the ups and downs.

The best you can look forward to is progress, not perfection. Fortunately, you are in control of your progress. The more you toe the line and do the exercises in this book, the more rapidly you can expect to see progress.

MINDFULNESS MEDITATION:
Befriend Your Emotions

Read these instructions to yourself, then put down the book and do the meditation.

1. Take a moment to sit back in your chair and get comfortable.

2. Close your eyes and, as you focus on your breath, feel the sensations in your heart. Allow yourself to recognize the emotions you are feeling at this very moment and embrace the full spectrum of what is possible.

3. Now remember a time when you felt at ease with your recovering partner. Take a moment to recall what that felt like, and then let it go.

4. Now remember a time when you felt scared of your recovering partner. Take a moment to recall what that felt like, and then let it go.

5. Now remember a time when you felt happy with your recovering partner. Take a moment to recall what that felt like, and then let it go.

6. Now remember a time when you felt sad with your recovering partner. Take a moment to recall what that felt like, and then let it go.

7. Allow yourself to embrace all the different emotional experiences you've had with your recovering partner as you breathe deeply into your heart. Let your feelings flow like a river and observe them with love and compassion, acceptance and nonjudgment.

8. Whenever you're ready, open your eyes and stay present.

Conclusion

Tuning in to your feelings when you would rather tune out, focusing on the world around you when you would rather indulge your bad moods, and learning to contemplate your feelings through writing and sitting still are skills that can benefit anybody. But not everybody needs to depend on these tools in the way a recovering codependent and his or her recovering addict partner do for their relationship to survive. That being true, remember: recovery is not about being Ms. or Mr. Perfect; it is about getting better and better at living in a real-world relationship, free from trauma and peril. When you do slip up and your moods or emotions upset your recovering partner, as they inevitably will, you now have the nifty mindfulness pointers from this chapter to help you move through a negative cycle or dynamic more quickly.

Initially, confronting mood difficulties can make you feel a bit like you're playing a game of Whack-A-Mole as you deal with a wide range of underlying issues. This is why taking a holistic approach is so important. Instead of whacking one mole at a time, you need to get the big picture and appreciate how all the physical, emotional, and mental aspects of your well-being are interrelated.

Along the way, your recovery may include an entire network of doctors, meditation teachers, gyms, spiritual advisors, and mentors. You don't need to get overwhelmed by this fact. Not everyone needs that much support to stay stable and happy, but some people do. Whether you require medication for a mood disorder, could benefit from a change in your diet or exercise routine, or wish to talk to a professional about PTSD, give yourself whatever you feel is necessary. Have no shame. It is more than fair to take advantage of any resources that can help you to better master your bad moods and negative emotions.

Simply put, if you take the time to improve your emotional, mental, and physical health, you will become more stable and robust before long. It is no fun for anyone to end up in a dry syndrome rampant with negative feelings. Even though every codependent is capable of operating in dry syndrome for long periods of time, it's always nice to know you aren't doomed to live there. If you don't have everything in place just yet, don't worry—you will. By taking small steps, you've already shown tremendous courage toward getting, and staying, on a path of healing.

CHAPTER 5

Rapport: Responding, Not Reacting

Being steadily on a path of recovery can transform your mentality so radically you no longer feel like the person you once were. For example, in the past, you might have patted yourself on the back if you won a fight or successfully avoided once again dealing with a long-standing issue with your recovering partner. Those days are over. The kind of self-congratulation that used to come with winning has not only gotten old in your relationship, it has gotten boring! You now want your conversations to flow more smoothly and nourish your heart mightily, so that your original purpose for sticking around can be achieved. You are looking to reap a much greater reward by becoming adept at creating a solid rapport with your recovering partner.

Rapport is a term that describes the sympathetic resonance between people who relate well to each other. It is a sense of togetherness that goes deeper than just keeping the peace or not upsetting each other. The art of sustaining rapport is mastered when you have the ability to pause long enough to know exactly where you are coming from in your reactions and how to negotiate those reactions collaboratively with your recovering partner. Without this, conversations at best are empty words accompanied by hollow feelings, and at worst can cause true hurt.

In a recovering relationship, rapport can be hard to sustain. To anyone looking at your relationship from the outside, some of the ways you relate to your partner might seem mysterious and irrational. But for you there is no mystery. You know whether a subtle movement of your partner's eyebrows, or even eyeballs, or a slight shrug is a warning. You know if you are safe or unsafe. If you feel unsafe, what do you do? You might withdraw, or you might attack. Either way, you react! As soon as you move into reactive mode, the usual signs and tools you use to stay connected become inaccessible. Rapport is lost.

What you need is a more reliable way to maintain rapport. We have already seen how mindfulness can make a big difference in how you feel in your relationship. The area in which mindfulness can help your relationship the most is communication. This chapter will show you how to mindfully increase the level of rapport in your relationship, and give you the tools to step away from reactivity and power struggles, to let go of resentment, and to increase your ability to feel gratitude.

Building Rapport

To build rapport in your relationship, you need to stop being so *reactive* and start being more *responsive*. That is the basic shift in communication style we're talking about here. Now, you may have pulled out your thesaurus and noticed the first synonym for "responsive" is "reactive." You're thinking, "Beverly, no splitting hairs, please!" But I say hold your horses; when it comes to your relationship, this is more than a semantic difference. Let's look at the practical differences.

To be reactive is to speak and act without a clear intention. It is about being rash, unthinking, and self-centered. It's about the tone and volume of your voice. When you are reactive, there are lots of exclamation marks at the end of your sentences (!!!!!) As a codependent, you readily fall into the knee-jerk reactions of arguing, defending, and shutting down. If you don't rein in such reactions, your conversations with your partner either escalate into full-blown battles or turn into cold wars. At these difficult moments, fear and reactivity can ignite and leave you feeling untrusting of your partner's motives, and even questioning whether you are loved at all.

Responsiveness is exactly the opposite. It is about being mindful, receptive, open, approachable, deliberate, and compassionate. It's like a cool cucumber, compared to the hot chili of reactivity. When you become mindful of the manner in which you speak, you can control your pitch and pace during conversations. This does not ensure you will never alienate your partner, or vice versa, but it sure does give you a better chance of creating connection, lowering fear, and getting control over reactivity.

Rapport Breakers/Reaction Makers

If you want to shift from being reactive to being responsive, a good place to start is by recognizing when you are being reactive to your recovering partner. The following statements represent some of the most common ways partners relate to each other that spark reactivity and loss of rapport:

- "You talk so loud it makes me cringe."

- "Your tone of voice is gruff and unloving."

- "You react quickly and talk too fast for me."

- "You whine."

- "You seem indifferent when you're talking to me."

- "You avoid me entirely when the conversation turns to something you don't want to talk about."

- "You are impatient with me and sound frustrated."

- "You don't look me in the eyes when you speak to me."

- "You're always so sarcastic."

- "You don't listen to me."

Do any of these sound familiar to you? If so, have you heard them spoken by your partner or coming out of your own mouth? Or both?

The thing about rapport breakers is that they don't just stop the conversation in the moment; they create a cycle of broken communication. That is why I also refer to them as reaction makers. One reaction leads to another. If one partner is reactive, the other partner is likely to respond in kind. For example, if you say to your partner, "You don't listen to me," your partner will probably feel defensive. Your statement will be a reaction maker for him or her, and the response you get is likely to be along the lines of "Well, how can you expect me to listen when you are always whining?" Or "I do listen. But you react way too quickly and you talk too fast. I can't keep up!"

A Culture of Reactivity

Your tendency to be reactive instead of responsive is not entirely your fault. We live in a culture in which it is getting harder and harder to give one another the full attention necessary to build rapport and nurture intimate relationships. In this world of digital distraction and information overload, listening is a skill we're in danger of losing. Technology has made us used to receiving immediate results in the form of sound bytes. We are so dependent on texting and e-mail that we easily get impatient if it takes too long for our partner to get a point across. We have practically stopped using face-to-face conversation as a way to know our partners. So not only are alienation and loneliness more common between partners, but reactivity is on the increase. Knowing this, you can protest against the culture at large interfering with your relationship by turning off your computer, putting down your phone, and devoting some time each day to connecting through listening to your partner.

I mention this because approaching the issue of communication in context can make it easier to build rapport. Instead of being part of the broader problem, you can be part of the solution.

TRY THIS: Mindful Listening

The first step to building rapport is to refuse to let your brain get the best of you in any conversation with your partner that would normally trigger unmanageable reactivity. This calls for restraint and mindful listening the moment you notice your blood pressure rising. Mindful listening is what leads to understanding. And understanding is what leads to rapport.

For example, your partner says, "I need to talk to you about the way we are spending money." Or "I need to talk to you about our sex life." Or "I need to talk to you about _____" (fill in the blank with whatever gets your goat). It feels as though your blood pressure is going up, up, up. Insight, understanding, and thoughtful speaking go out the window.

This is when you need to apply mindful listening. Your mission is to do the following:

Stop in your tracks.

Breathe.

Be still.

Listen to your own heartbeat.

Do not do anything else until you relax and feel back in control again.

Resume your conversation.

You may notice the similarity here to the mindful walk-away from chapter 3. In fact, they are cousins. If it takes too long for you to get back in control, you may want to do a walk-away. However, as you practice mindful listening, you will find it takes less and less time to regain control. It may be only a matter of seconds before you're able to return to the conversation in a responsive, not reactive, manner.

You may feel you and your partner are miles away from having skill at mindful listening, but I'm going to show you that over time it is quite attainable. I'm not suggesting that you start curtseying before you speak or stifling your expression in unnatural ways. Having rich and meaningful conversations is a realistic goal if you are willing to start taking an honest look at how well you practice going from reaction to response, and if you work at mindfully listening to your partner when he or she is talking.

TRY THIS: Break Your Reactive Pattern Without the Help of Your Recovering Partner

One good thing about becoming a change agent in your relationship, as we discussed in chapter 3, is that you can create change with or without your partner's help. Whatever you're doing, though, it helps to be transparent with your recovering partner so that he or she doesn't become suspicious when you suddenly seem to be morphing into a different person for no apparent reason.

Before you start this exercise, tell your partner you're reading a book that is teaching you about mindfulness, and for the next week you are going to practice being especially mindful of how you react when the two of you interact. Say you'll be watching what triggers you to react negatively during face-to-face conversations and over texts and e-mails. Explain that you are working to get control over your reactivity and to keep your cool in the face of it.

Know that just by telling your recovering partner this, you have already begun to make a change in the way you relate. Plus, putting your partner on alert may spark his or her own responsiveness.

Over the next week, notice the kinds of reactions that come up for you when you and your recovering partner are in contact with each other. Ask yourself the following questions, and jot down your observations. This will not only help you get better acquainted with your own reactivity, but start to reveal the ongoing dynamics between you and your partner.

- *When do you want to flee?*

- *When do you want to aggress?*

- *When do you feel steady? Centered? Grounded? On your game?*

If at any moment a negative reaction arises, pause and take some mindful breaths. Say to yourself, "Hello. I am reacting now." See if you can breathe into the sensations, sustain the conversation, and stay in neutral.

As you get better at doing this, you will gain the ability to bounce back to a calm state after getting reactive with your partner. You'll feel much more in control of yourself. You may even look forward to having a fight-or-flight reaction just so you can test your ability to calm yourself down.

Believe it or not, your brain will stop protecting you the way a guard dog would. Instead, you're giving it a new command: "Down, brain, down!"

Question: "Why Does My Partner Still React with So Much Aggression Even Though He or She Is in Recovery?"

Lucy and Albert were in their early thirties and had been together for three years when Lucy went into rehab for drug and alcohol abuse. During treatment, she made promises in front of both her chemical dependency counselor and Albert about what she would do to stay sober when she got home. In addition to staying sober, one promise was to work on controlling her knee-jerk reactions during their conflicts. Albert, on the other hand, agreed to break his habit of either being falsely compliant or fleeing when Lucy was reactive.

However, despite their best intentions, Lucy continued to have outbursts, and Albert continued to run or back down at the first sign of conflict. The last straw for them was when Lucy threw a glass across the room during one of their fights, and it shattered. Obviously things had gone way too far. They decided to seek therapy.

During our first meeting, Lucy openly admitted, "I can be very self-righteous and angry when Albert upsets me. I know it shows a lack of regard for him, but I can't help it. The problem is, now that I'm sober, I feel shame like I never did before when I lost control of myself. Honestly, it's demoralizing. I guess I'm not only powerless over my drinking, but over my reactions as well. As they say in AA meetings, 'I surrender.'"

Although Lucy was making herself vulnerable, Albert was not yet able to take it in. With pleading eyes and in a small voice, he asked, "Why does Lucy still react to me with so much aggression even though she is sober now?"

I answered, "Simply put, when Lucy gets scared or angry, you become her enemy. She's telling you the truth: she hasn't learned how to get control over herself when she gets distressed. She is *talking* like a recovering person, but is not yet able to *act* like one. Fortunately, she's taken the first step by admitting she is powerless over her behavior."

Albert's defensive posture appeared to drop as he exhaled, but he was far from truly trusting. How could he be sure Lucy's admittance of defeat was going to give her more control in the future when she got upset? He said, "I appreciate what Lucy's saying, but I need to see her handling her upset feelings differently before I can trust her. But whether she does or not, I don't want to keep reacting the way I have been, either. I feel demoralized, as well."

You may be experiencing something similar in your own relationship. It is very important that you know how to stand up for yourself and how to protect yourself in the face of a reactive attack by your recovering partner. You may have to fight your own strong urge to make nice, run away, or continue making excuses for your recovering partner's negative behavior. These behaviors are all rapport breakers that will do nothing more than trigger further reactions. Instead, you have to take a stand and discover a new level of courage. That means pausing and bringing mindfulness to your conversations with your recovering partner. The following exercise can help lay the groundwork for that.

TRY THIS: Mindful Visualization for Self-Empowerment

This mindful meditation is designed to show you the power your mind has to design your reality. Begin by finding a quiet location where you won't be disturbed for a few moments.

1. Take a comfortable sitting position and close your eyes.

2. Concentrate on your breathing. With each breath you take, see if you can observe all the sensations in your body, all your thoughts, and all your emotions, just as they are right now.

3. Now imagine having a loving conversation with your partner about a difficult subject. It could be finances, child rearing, sex, or any subject that strains your relationship.

4. Imagine the conversation going exactly as you wish it would in real life.

5. If either of you says something you don't like, quickly alter the scenario. Remember, your mind has the power to imagine anything you want it to.

6. Sink into a gentle awareness that change is possible and that you can feel secure in your relationship with your recovering partner.

7. Whenever you're ready, open your eyes and stay present with yourself.

Of course, imagining this reality won't automatically alter your next conversation with your partner. However, bringing the feeling of empowerment you felt while doing this visualization into your next communication with your partner can be an important first step in building rapport.

Three Styles of Communication

When we look at Albert and Lucy, we see two styles of communication: Albert's reactive running away and Lucy's reactive attack mode. Both are styles they developed at an early age.

Albert's parents were distant and critical. If Albert misbehaved as a child, his father made him feel ashamed by expressing deep disappointment. As he got older, his parents gave swift, harsh consequences if he disobeyed them. This left him feeling insecure and anxious. His relationship with Lucy was driven by his fear of conflict and of potential rejection and judgment. Lucy's parents, on the other hand, were unpredictable. The only time she felt close to her father was when she was old enough to drink, and they shared a bottle of wine together. This left Lucy angry and ambivalent. She later brought these feelings to her relationship with Albert.

In fact, these two styles are typical of many partners, especially recovering codependents and addicts.

Do you identify with either of the following sets of statements?

1. Albert's anxious style:

   - I'm afraid to make my recovering partner consider my feelings for fear he or she will reject me.

   - It's hard for me to trust my recovering partner and to invest more of myself emotionally.

   - I don't know what my needs are, and I get anxious when trying to consider them in the face of my recovering partner.

2. Lucy's ambivalent style:

   - I feel distressed when I need my recovering partner emotionally.

   - I don't trust that my recovering partner really wants to be with me.

   - I want to be close with my recovering partner, but I feel angry with him or her much of the time.

If the first communication style sounds like you, as you get better at asserting your feelings and stop holding back, you will build a more secure base with your recovering partner. If the second communication style sounds like you, your focus should be on letting yourself be more vulnerable, as Lucy expressed in our therapy session. Yes, your basic communication style was developed early in life, and may be hard to overcome, but with a mindful approach you can change it for the better.

There is a third communication style, as well, exemplified by the following statements:

- I am not here to compete with my partner to win; I am here to be close.

- Without my allowing both of our voices to be respected in the relationship, there is no "we."

- Even in the face of my own reactivity, I trust that our relationship will endure.

If this sounds like you, know that you are in second stage recovery and well on the way to building rapport between you and your partner.

TRY THIS: Create a Mindful Communication Style

I suggest that you develop a mindful communication style you think will work for you. If you do this, you will start to feel more confident in your ability to be responsive instead of reactive.

Read the following statements and select ones you want to incorporate into your mindful communication style. If you have statements that would suit your style better, feel free to add those. Write down all the statements that together make up the unique mindful communication style of your choice. This is an exercise you can do alone or with your recovering partner. You will benefit from it either way.

1. I speak in a loving tone of voice, even when the subject we are discussing is provoking me into a fight-or-flight reaction.

2. I am very careful before I speak my mind when I feel upset.

3. I notice when either of us looks sad or scared during an especially difficult conversation, and I stop the conversation to check in with my partner.

4. I ask for a walk-away when a conversation has gotten too heated and I am in a fight-or-flight reaction.

5. I know when my fight-or-flight reaction has calmed down and I am ready to reach out to my partner again.

6. When I become reactive in a conversation, I know when to sit close to my partner and gaze into his or her eyes and when to take my gaze away.

7. I know the exact moment to take a break from a conversation that is starting to go downhill and igniting my fight-or-flight reaction.

8. I respect when my partner requests that I lower my voice, calm down, or slow down because I am contributing to his or her fight-or-flight reaction.

9. I am acutely aware of when my anxiety level goes up during a conversation.

10. I hug my partner after successfully completing a difficult conversation and getting back in sync with each other.

11. I express myself with statements such as "I'm starting to get reactive and I want to run," or "I'm starting to get reactive and too aggressive."

12. I respectfully stop what I am doing without hesitation or argument when my partner expresses distress during a conversation.

13. I apologize after stepping on my partner's toes in a heated conversation.

14. I say out loud to my partner before I begin a difficult conversation that I will monitor my reactivity, and I agree to stop immediately when I get reactive.

15. I talk in a whisper after my reactive style gets ignited.

16. I talk in a neutral tone after my reactive style gets ignited.

17. I talk slowly and at a normal volume after my reactive style gets ignited.

18. I openly agree to stop talking and breathe after getting caught up in a power struggle with my partner.

19. I sit far enough away from my partner during difficult conversations to protect my reactive style from getting ignited.

20. I stop, breathe, and calm down so that I can think carefully about my partner's position before my reactive style ignites.

21. When my partner makes a point, I check that I have understood correctly before moving on. For example: "Let me see if I have this right. Are you saying _____?"

22. I do not let my communication style to get in the way of allowing my partner to have different points of view, emotions, and opinions.

As you construct your ideal, mindful communication style, honestly recognize where your habitual communication style may have been ineffective in the past. I don't mean beat yourself up for how you've been communicating—I just mean be straight up and accountable for your side of the street. The ability to do this is very important for you, as a recovering codependent, to be able to grow.

I asked Albert and Lucy to create their own mindful communication styles that would carry them into second stage recovery. Albert replaced his old reactions with new mindful responses, and with time, his flight reaction to conflict was in his control. His newfound ability to hold on to his own ideas and feelings in the face of Lucy's now-tempered anger gave him a confidence he had never known before.

Lucy's days of throwing things in angry fits, and Albert's days of crouching behind a bush in fear, were over. In their place were robust self-expression and solid connection even during arguments.

Regardless of how your communication style has gotten you into trouble—whether you've been avoidant or argumentative—you can get back to your connection if you get a grip on yourself and begin implementing the statements you've chosen for your new mindful communication style. If your recovering partner is not interested in creating one with you, it doesn't matter. Just hang on tight to yours. It's hard to have a combative conversation with someone who refuses to have one. And that someone could be you.

Do I Have to Surrender?

The addict isn't the only one who has to surrender to a recovering life on a daily basis. So does the codependent.

What does it mean to "surrender," anyway? For the codependent, it means to cease trying to be in control of your recovering partner. The practice of mindfully sitting with any thoughts or feelings of powerlessness that come from giving up control over others is an act of surrender. Make a list of the ways you wish you had control over your recovering partner, your relationship, or your circumstances. For each item on your list, mentally say to yourself, *For today, I am letting go of trying to control this.*

Some people think surrender is a sign of weakness. It's not! Surrendering doesn't mean you are being selfish or giving up on your recovering partner; it means you are calming your reactivity and giving yourself the space to delve into your humanity at a deeper level. Surrendering old ideas—such as thinking you know better than your recovering partner what is good for him or her, and letting go of the reins—takes great humility. It also takes faith that there's something out there worth giving those things up for. The recovering partner you love has to surrender his or her addiction, and you have to surrender indiscriminately helping your partner. Thus, surrender is a building block of good rapport.

Question: "I'm Glad My Partner Is Finally in Recovery, but I Can't Stop Resenting Him or Her. What Should I Do?"

Betsy had been through hell and back dealing with Ted's compulsive debting and constant lying about finances in their relationship. Ted had abstained from compulsive debting for six months. He was going to Debtors Anonymous meetings twice a week, had a sponsor to work the 12 steps with, and had joined a pressure relief group. Although Ted had owned up to his process addiction, Betsy and Ted were still not out of the woods. They hadn't had sex in three months, and Betsy was so filled with resentment she could barely look Ted in the eye when they spoke. They were unable to get out of a vicious cycle in which Betsy felt ignored and ended up yelling and crying, leading Ted to go mute, which only infuriated Betsy more. Betsy said, "I'm glad Ted is finally in recovery, but I can't stop resenting him, and I know this is making it nearly impossible for us to connect. What should I do?"

I said, "Recovery is a great igniter of hope; however, your hope needs to be based on realistic expectations." I explained to Betsy that she had to get a handle on her resentment if things were to improve between her and Ted. Equally critical was the ability to apologize. To build rapport between them, Betsy and Ted needed to learn to mindfully listen to each other. But even that would be difficult without knowing how to handle resentment and how to apologize. I suggested they start there.

How Resentment Acts as a Roadblock to Rapport

If you identify with Betsy, you may not have had time to consider the resentments building up inside of you. You've been too busy changing the lock on your front door, closing checking accounts you had with your partner, or running around town at all hours of the night calling out your partner's name. You may have surrendered to codependent recovery, but you nonetheless find yourself left with a backlog of hurt feelings to heal, betrayals to process, and resentments to address.

Every time you and your recovering partner try to talk, the resentments you harbor toward him or her create roadblocks to your rapport. You can't seem to move forward together. Instead of listening to your partner, you speak—if not yell—from a place of resentment. Resentment colors your words with anger and frustration and sarcasm. How can you expect your partner not to react to all that?

If you want to stop this vicious cycle, it is incumbent on you to find a way to walk the fine line between denying that you still hold resentments and being willing to finally let them go. You can do this by actively requesting that your partner make certain changes in his or her behavior. Remember boundaries? However, the most foolproof way is to process those resentments within yourself. Again, your recovering partner doesn't need to know every move you're making. And that includes moves you make for the benefit of the relationship.

I suggested that Betsy try the following gratitude exercise, and she found it useful for releasing resentments and calming her negative reactions to Ted. I know hundreds of codependents who attest that writing a daily gratitude list significantly reduced their anger and resentment, even when their recovering partner continued to do the same things that usually drove them up a tree.

TRY THIS: Invoke Gratitude
to Dissolve Resentment

Write down five things you are grateful for in your life.

Now write down five things you are grateful for about your recovering partner.

Do this for thirty days in a row.

If it doesn't work after thirty days, you can stop doing it. All I ask is that you don't pooh-pooh something before you've tried it.

And why, you wonder, should gratitude make a difference?

Here's the secret. Resentment only has a grip on you if you think someone owes you something. When you feel grateful for what you already have, resentment suddenly has a hard time finding something into which it can sink its teeth.

The Anatomy of an Apology

Ted continued to stay sober, and Betsy remained dedicated to writing a daily gratitude list and practicing mindful meditation. Betsy would be the first to tell you that while all their hard work was finally paying off, one simple practice was a game changer.

Being able to apologize to your partner when he or she feels hurt by you is essential for building rapport. Yet I have found this is one of the hardest things for recovering addicts and codependents to incorporate into their daily lives. When I investigate further, I find that most people's parents never apologized to them in earnest, if at all, and didn't teach them the value of a sincere apology. In fact, apologizing is a way of repairing small tears that occur in rapport along the way, and bringing connection back. It isn't about one-upmanship, power plays, or domination.

Let's look at the makings of effective apologies.

Part One: When your partner says that something you did upset him or her, simply say, "I'm sorry."

Feeling ashamed because you did something hurtful is not a reason to avoid apologizing. Nor is the fact that your partner also hurt you. You may want to say to your partner, "Well, you did it to me! Why should I apologize?" But it's not about tit for tat.

If you think your partner is being unfair or hypersensitive, that's fine, but say you are sorry anyway. And say it immediately, as you would to a stranger you accidentally bumped into on the street. No argument. Just, "Oh, I'm sorry." When you apologize quickly, you prevent the build-up of resentment in your partner.

Of course, you have the right to a mindful walk-away after the apology.

Part Two: When your partner apologizes for something he or she did that upset you, accept your partner's apology immediately. Then just drop it and move on.

If you're a master at harboring a grudge, now is the time to break that habit. Your partner's apology may seem weak or insincere, but that doesn't give you license to reject him or her for weeks on end.

Later, you have permission to say gently, "Can we slow down a minute and try it again? I'm not connecting with the way you've chosen to say you're sorry." But initially just say, "Thank you." You have total permission to use the walk-away in this case, too.

Recovery and Communication

As a child of the sixties, I'm all for freedom of speech and self-expression. But until your resentments have been laid to rest and your reactivity is under control, I'm going to ask you to forget about being spontaneous when it comes to expressing yourself to your recovering partner. Instead of spontaneity, let's go for strengthening your skills at bringing mindfulness to your communication. For example, continue to hold back before you give your partner an opinion or advice he or she hasn't asked for yet.

I understand that you may have moments when you're so overwhelmed with hurt or hostile feelings toward your recovering partner that you can't find even the smallest bit of love for him or her. The Buddha gave a beautiful teaching about offering loving-kindness toward others called the *Mettā Sutta*. The good news is that you don't have to become a Buddhist monk to practice this meditation for abandoning negative feelings and cultivating positive ones. The following is a simplified version, which you can do easily.

MINDFULNESS MEDITATION:
Mindfully Send Loving-Kindness to Your Recovering Partner

Imagine your good feelings as a helium balloon on a string. If you let go of the string, the balloon will float to the ceiling. It may bob around out of reach, but the balloon is not gone. This meditation will help your mind grab the string and pull those loving feelings back into your reach. There are many ways of dealing with angry feelings toward your recovering partner, but let's start with this one.

1. Sit comfortably somewhere you can be alone for two minutes without disruption.

2. Close your eyes and imagine your partner in your mind's eye.

3. Think to yourself: *I wish the best for my recovering partner. I wish for him or her what he or she wishes for himself or herself. I hope my partner's future is fulfilling and happy and brings great peace. May my partner be well, happy, and peaceful. May no harm come to my partner. May no*

difficulties come to my partner. May no problems come to my partner. May my partner always meet with success. May my partner also have patience, courage, understanding, and determination to meet and overcome inevitable difficulties, problems, and failures in life.

Do this meditation each day. You can even do it several times a day. See for yourself if it softens your heart. And remember that you can be very angry with your partner even as you feel love for and wish him or her well.

Conclusion

Just as the inability to manage moods and emotions can take a great toll on your relationship, so too can the inability to communicate mindfully and let go of resentments. The formula you want to use instead looks something like this: loving self-control + discerning self-expression + mindfulness = a kinder and gentler connection with your partner, and ultimately a more collaborative partnership. In other words, good rapport. I promise you, you can feel confident that conversations with your partner need never again feel like treacherous territory.

As you continue to be mindful in your communication, the reign of your ambivalent or anxious style will be over and a secure style will take its place. Responsive communicators have a solid sense of their own values and respect, without necessarily agreeing with, the values of their partner. They are able to listen well and come back to a relaxed and present state when conflicts arise. When responsive communicators feel any negativity toward their partner, they know how to express it in ways that are helpful, not hurtful. Responsive communicators will not stand for abusive relationships. To this end, they work hard to create an atmosphere of cooperation with their partner and are more interested in connection, rather than simply fighting to be right, as the goal of communication.

Your efforts at consciously creating the rules of the game, gaining control over your reactivity, and being prompt with apology will eventually change the negative dynamics with which you've been struggling, and strong lines of rapport will take their place. You will start to believe that you and your recovering partner can be close, trust each other, and feel secure.

Just as we all have a desire to be happy and a need for love and connection, none of us can escape the fact that emotional pain is part of life. This is especially true for those working hard on issues of addiction in a committed partnership. The truth is, entering recovery gives addicts, and the partners who love them, a golden opportunity to clean up their act and achieve the kind of rapport they long for. It isn't easy to regain the best of yourself after being held hostage by reactivity, but with enough effort you will. The prize for your efforts will be a resurrected love for your recovering partner and a newfound respect for yourself.

CHAPTER 6

Intimacy and Desire: Bringin' Sexy Back

Although sex is complicated for most couples in a long-term relationship, it can be even more complicated for you as a member of a couple recovering from addiction and codependency. You may have to find creative ways to escape humdrum sex, fight against dwindling desire, and reconcile disparate sexual styles. And as if that weren't enough, getting over sexual and emotional betrayal and resolving historical trauma and old resentments are also real and serious issues that you may need to face in recovery.

Negotiating about sex can be intimidating when both partners are in recovery. Who wants to feel ashamed for wanting more sex, or less sex, or kinky sex? You may still have a libidinal supply, but attempting to make use of it now that you are truly naked before one another can feel like your awkward adolescence all over again. Or maybe the sex you're having is just dull and monotonous now that you're looking down a well of no desire.

Between children, heavy work schedules, and following a recovery program, it is not uncommon to be more overcome with exhaustion than with passion. Perhaps you desperately try to feel a want for your recovering partner, but you just can't. Or vice versa. Give yourself a chance to find desire and sexual expression in new and different ways before you come to any premature conclusions about your relationship.

If you are squeamish about the subject of sex, or simply don't feel ready to deal with the issue, feel free to skip this chapter. Or try challenging yourself to tolerate your discomfort in exchange for the possibility of creating a better sex life with your recovering partner. Either way, sooner or later, you'll have to deal with your sex life if you want to sustain interest, desire, and eroticism long term. If you do decide to take the plunge, please put a moratorium on self-judgment as you explore what you desire or fantasize about sexually, the amount of sex you want, and whatever sexual difficulties you are having with your partner. I guarantee it is possible to transform what may feel like a hopeless situation into a hopeful one by taking a few simple steps.

I also recommend that you don't judge your recovering relationship against any other couple's relationship. You never know what really goes on behind other couples' bedroom doors. Many couples have a thorn in the side of their sex life that could use some tending to. So instead, let's start investigating you. Regardless of the current shape of your sex life, recovery gives you the chance to pull back the covers, turn on the lights, open your eyes, and start getting more connection and pleasure in bed with your recovering partner.

Your Sexuality in Recovery

It can feel as if recovery has turned the high beams on your sex life. The potential for sex to be mediocre, bad, or downright awful runs high when you are in recovery together for the first time (even for the second, third, or fourth time, for that matter). You may feel you don't know how to get from the front door into the bedroom anymore. Or if you can get to the bedroom, you may not know what to do once you get there!

The scary thing about sex in recovery is that it exposes you to your recovering partner in a way that the haze of addiction and codependency never allowed. You are now exposed to daunting emotional vulnerability, body image issues, and fears of sexual incompetence and rejection. But as long as you can brave your feelings while addressing these issues, you can be confident you will come out stronger and your sex life will be better as a result.

Sex is a very personal matter. The touchy, or not so touchy, subject of sex—which for some couples has become increasingly less "touchy" in the literal sense—is an important piece of the puzzle to a hearty relationship. Therefore, before you even get undressed, you need to know what you like and don't like, want and don't want, to do with your recovering partner in the bedroom. I suggest that you begin with a mindfulness meditation and an exercise that will help you clarify this focus.

MINDFULNESS MEDITATION:
Your Own Sexuality

Read these instructions to yourself, then put down the book and do the meditation.

1. Close your eyes. Take a deep breath in and a long, slow breath out, and allow yourself to relax. Notice where you are holding tension in your body. Breathe into those places and allow yourself to relax more fully.

2. As you continue breathing, allow yourself to become aware of your sexuality. Notice any pleasant as well as any uncomfortable sensations that arise in your body.

3. Ask yourself, "How do I see myself as a sexual being?"

4. Next ask yourself, "If I could have any kind of sex life with my recovering partner, what would it be like?" Notice what sensations, thoughts, emotions, and images arise as you ponder this question.

5. As you continue to relax, let each breath take you deeper into a state of curiosity about the future of your sex life. Breathe in the possibility of what you would like in your sex life. Breathe out any resistance you have to your sex life being exactly as it is at this moment.

6. Whenever you feel ready, open your eyes.

TRY THIS: Bring Mindfulness to Your Sex Life

To be clear about what you would like your sex life to look like in the future, it is important to take into account the totality of your experience. You may have been aware of being a sexual creature from a very early age. Or perhaps you didn't awaken to sexuality until you reached adolescence, or even adulthood. You may still feel you haven't begun to fully understand who you are as a sexual person. Regardless of where you are on this spectrum, you can now step into your sexuality in a more mindful way. I suggest that you begin by considering the influence of your upbringing, the culture you grew up in, and the sexual experiences you have gone through.

As you review the following questions, be mindful of the feelings, thoughts, and sensations you are experiencing. Take your time to think about each answer. If you are so inclined, write your thoughts down in your journal.

- *Where did you first learn about sex?*

- *Do you have sexual abuse in your history? If yes, what have you done to address it?*

- *How would you describe your sexual history with your recovering partner?*

- *What do you consider "good sex"? "Mediocre sex"? "Bad sex"?*

- *What are your most frequent sexual fantasies?*

- *Who wants sex more often in your relationship?*

- *How is sex initiated between you and your partner? Do you like it this way?*

- *Has there been sexual infidelity in your relationship? If so, how was it addressed?*

- *What has inhibited you from being fearlessly honest with your partner about what you like sexually?*

- *How have fear and resentment interfered with your ability to enjoy sex with your recovering partner?*

- *Do you like sex? Why? Why not?*

- *How could sex be better with your recovering partner in the future?*

Sexuality Through the Ages

If we look at historical Judeo-Christian influences, the Bible has had an enormous role in teaching people how to live righteously, ethically, and compassionately. It also was the first Western doctrine that decreed how a couple should behave sexually. Sinful sex included homosexuality, erotica, bisexuality, friends with benefits, adultery, swinging, prostitution, sinful lust, and pornography. The Bible defines normal by characterizing coupledom behavior as good or evil, and right or wrong, based on how closely people adhere to strict codes and ethics.

I mention the doctrine pertaining to sex in the Bible because these codes are swimming in the undercurrent of our culture and our sub-conscious minds even today. You might want to consider giving yourself the space to consciously rule out judging your sexual proclivities as good or evil. At the end of the day, every recovering couple should enjoy being fully expressive, without shame or self-rejection, in all areas of their life, including their sex life. Besides, with all the widespread and rapidly changing sexual mores, who is to say what is normal or abnormal? I suggest moving forward by focusing on whether you are satisfied or unsatisfied with your sex life. For example, you may not have sex with your recovering partner very often and feel frustrated by that. Or your partner may want sex every day of the week, and you feel pressured by that. Both circumstances are a problem simply because they leave you feeling dissatisfied. Again, there is no right or wrong here, only dissatisfaction.

Question: "My Partner and I Used to Have Great Sex. What Do I Do Now That He or She Is in Recovery and Rarely Wants It?"

When I met George and Kathy, they had been together six years. Kathy, thirty-three years old, had ten months in recovery from daily pot smoking and drinking, and was going to Narcotics Anonymous meetings twice a week. George, twenty-nine years old, had started going to Al-Anon meetings six months before Kathy quit using. They came to see me in hopes of figuring out why their sex life had gone down the tubes shortly after Kathy got clean and sober. Neither had any history of sexual trauma, and neither had been unfaithful in the relationship.

George was clearly feeling the sting of rejection. "After going to Al-Anon, I started praying for Kathy to get clean and sober," he said, "but as weird as this may sound, there are days I wish she would just smoke a little pot so we could have our old sex life back." Behind his sadness, there was anger, too. He was tired of patiently waiting for Kathy to want sex with him more often, and he had gotten to the point of threatening to look elsewhere. In turn, Kathy felt she was being asked to "cough up more sex" to hold on to him. "I don't even know if Kathy desires me anymore. I'm beginning to wonder if she ever did," George said angrily. "Kathy and I used to have great sex. What do I do now that she is in recovery and rarely wants it?"

In fact, you may not know until your partner gets into recovery exactly where your respective levels of desire stand. I know it can be painful to repeatedly fight because your sexual needs aren't met. No one needs to tell you how anxiety provoking it can be to have your partner constantly demanding more sex than you want to give. It is no less painful if your partner is depriving you of the amount of sex you want. Either way, you are left thinking, "What's wrong with my partner?" Or "What's wrong with me?" It is common for differing desires for sex to throw a wrench into the recovery process.

Many factors affect our level of sexual desire. The five factors I see most often in couples in recovery—and that I encouraged George and Kathy to examine as they worked on their relationship—are issues related to (a) self-approval; (b) differences in sexual style preferences; (c) no desire or low desire; (d) fear of intimacy; and (e) the past (historical trauma or infidelity, for example). Let's look at how each of these plays out in your relationship, and what you can do about it.

This will require a generosity of spirit and willingness to explore any roadblocks in the way of a more thriving sex life. However, once again, you can make significant progress even without your partner's overt cooperation.

Self-Approval over Partner Approval

Like George, you may feel that your sex life was better while your partner was in the midst of his or her addiction. This is because active addiction and codependency numb out self-conscious and anxious feelings, making it easy to ignore underlying problems, such as your constant need for your partner's approval. When you enter recovery from codependency, you suddenly face the challenges you were avoiding. You can no longer avoid uncomfortable conversations.

For example, Kathy had always been afraid to tell George she didn't enjoy the ways he tried to initiate sex. She was overly dependent on his approval, and she feared that expressing her needs would cause him to reject her. It was easier to reject him first. However, as she progressed in her recovery, Kathy was able to state her feelings: "I don't like to be pawed at or treated like a sex object. You say you feel unloved when I don't jump at your first move. And if I do warm up, you keep asking every ten seconds if I like what you're doing. When I was high, I could ignore what turned me off and your constant need for my approval, but I can't anymore."

Kathy's shift away from excessive dependency on George left him unable to rely solely on her for approval as a man and as a lover. Instead, he needed to look within himself to cultivate self-love and self-approval.

In this instance, it was Kathy, the recovering addict, who initiated the break from codependency. However, you can't assume that will happen in your relationship. Remember, you have made a decision to be the agent of change in your relationship, whether your partner knows it or not!

The first step is to be honest with yourself. Ask yourself:

- To what extent am I comfortable with my own self-approval?

- To what extent am I vulnerable to my partner's disapproval?

- When am I most swayed by my partner's approval or lack thereof?

- How does the dance of approval and self-approval play out in our bedroom?

When you have acknowledged the role of approval in your relationship, you are ready for the next step. If you were overly dependent on your partner's approval and now find that approval is no longer automatically forthcoming, you will need to crank up your level of self-approval. Why? Because otherwise you won't be able to let go and introduce anything into your sex life that you fear may invite a critical eye from your partner. This leaves you with a secretive life in your fantasy world, and a lot of frustration in reality.

For example, suppose you want to dance naked with your partner as foreplay, but he or she won't even do that fully clothed. Or you want the lights on so that you can have eye contact while you talk dirty to each other, but your partner is only comfortable with the lights off and no talking. Avoiding your partner's disapproval in these cases means you have to ignore your own desires. If you and your partner are too anxious to experiment outside your sexual comfort zones, and you each accommodate yourself to the other's sexual bandwidth, your sex will be whittled down to a very narrow range. It will be short-lived, predictable sex that may protect you from embarrassment and anxiety, but end up extremely mechanical and leave you bored and unsatisfied.

The way to reclaim your identity as a sexual person and increase your chances of really having fun together is to cultivate what you enjoy sexually while taking the focus away from whether your partner approves of you. As the change agent in your relationship, you may start by talking dirty with the lights off, then turn the lights on when your partner gets more comfortable. Dancing naked may not happen until after your partner is comfortable dancing with clothes on. The point is to slowly introduce those things you haven't been doing only because you felt the need to avoid a disapproving look from your partner. I am not suggesting that you try anything that would lead your partner to feel violated in any way. I am simply proposing that you take steps to overcome the anxiety and fear of disapproval that has been inhibiting your sex life.

If you can see yourself as an advocate for greater expression of your sexuality, even in the face of your partner's potential disapproval, you will gain autonomy and self-approval. This does not mean your partner will necessarily be on board with everything that turns you on, but at least you'll know you have revealed yourself and aren't keeping your deepest wants secret. As you do the following meditation, remember that practicing being nonjudgmental will create a new basis for approval of yourself and acceptance of your partner. Suspending judgment is always important, but perhaps nowhere as notably as in the bedroom.

MINDFULNESS MEDITATION:
Reclaim Your Sexuality

Read these instructions to yourself, then put down the book and do the visualization.

1. Close your eyes. Take a deep breath in and a long, slow breath out, and allow yourself to relax.

2. Picture your recovering partner in your mind's eye. Be present with what you see. Watch, watch, watch!

3. Actively evoke a feeling of love toward your partner. Allow yourself to feel desire for your partner. Allow yourself to need your partner. As you do this, rest in your sense of self-approval.

4. Now imagine making love with your partner. Let yourself fantasize doing something you would like to do sexually with your partner, but that he or she might not find comfortable. As you do this, remember to breathe and calm yourself.

5. Allow yourself to enjoy what you want to enjoy, and imagine yourself being brave in the face of any response from your partner. Say to yourself, "My sexuality is mine. What I like, I like. What I want, I want. Whether my partner is game or not, I can still accept who I am, completely and totally. I am now ready, willing, and able to let go of my fear and replace it with courage."

6. When you open your eyes, hold a centered feeling and take a moment to be proud of yourself for reclaiming your sexuality.

Sexual Style Preferences

Disparate sexual style preferences are another factor that affects couples' level of sexual desire. Your recovering partner may not be on the same page as you with respect to what gets his or her wheels of desire turning. For example, you may feel aroused even before the act of sex begins, while your partner may not become aroused until you've started fooling around. What turns you on may be far afield from what turns your partner on.

Making the effort to be more open with your partner about your sexual preferences is an important step toward creating a better sex life together and finding true self-acceptance in the depths of your heart. It's often difficult to discuss your different levels of desire and your respective preferences without speaking to each other face to face. Maintaining rapport as you negotiate sexual preferences is just as important as maintaining rapport during any other negotiation. Negotiation has to be done cautiously, kindly, and with an open heart. If it is not carried out sensitively, you can end up being hurtful toward each other, requiring you to spend precious time tending to wounded feelings when you could be getting on with getting it on.

TRY THIS: Mindfully Talking About Sexual Preferences

As the change agent in your relationship, try initiating a conversation with your partner about your sex life. Here are some tips:

1. Pick a time when you are both relaxed and have no other distractions. Sit comfortably. I don't suggest having this conversation in the bedroom. If you feel rattled from the moment you sit down, just be mindful of that.

2. Tell your partner you want to approach the subject of sex in a spirit of love and collaboration, and hope he or she can offer the same in return. Agree to stay inside of a curious state together.

3. Use the following questions to guide your discussion. Some may feel too scary at this time. If none are suitable, feel free to come up with your own.

   - *What did you find most enjoyable about sex with me at the beginning of our relationship?*

   - *Are you comfortable with the amount of sex we are having?*

   - *If you felt no pressure at all, how often would you want sex with me?*

   - *Was there a time in our relationship you would say sex was great for you? In what way?*

   - *Do you think resentment or mistrust is affecting our sexual desire for each other?*

   - *Which of the ways I initiate sex do you like?*

   - *Are there any things I do during sex that you would prefer I do differently?*

   - *What do you need in order to feel safe to open up and experiment sexually with me?*

- *Do you know what I need in order to feel safe to open up and experiment sexually with you?*

- *Do you have any sexual abuse in your history that you have not dealt with yet?*

4. Give yourself permission to take as long as you and your partner need to discuss these questions. You don't need to get too far in one conversation. What matters most is that you open up about dissatisfactions and wants without World War III erupting.

5. Pause if something either of you says is upsetting. Remember, the walk-away is at your fingertips.

6. Keep talking. By that, I mean have more conversations about sex. I know this may be easier said than done, but you need to start talking about the elephant in the room. What better time than now?

When Sex Has Gone Out the Window

Maybe you are not having sex at all. Some experts say that if you and your partner have stopped having sex and aren't happy about that, then "just do it!" "Just doing it" looks like this: "Honey, I know we haven't been having sex, but if we don't just do it now, we may not do it ever. Can we break the ice and jump into the deep end of the pool together?" While this advice might seem counterintuitive, or even insensitive, the point is to try something radical to get out of the vicious cycle in which you are caught. If you are just sitting there frustrated, waiting to feel more connected to your partner before you have sex again, you might be waiting until the cows come home.

Is it good for you to have sex? The answer is yes. When you have sex, a hormone called *oxytocin* is released. Oxytocin makes you feel good, increases feelings of empathy and trust, and bonds you with your partner. Should you push yourself to have sex when you don't want to? Strangely, the answer is sometimes yes, and other times no. Even as an expert on marriage, I cannot tell you when you should force yourself to have sex. But I have seen the "just do it!" strategy work so much of the time that I can't help but resort to it when a couple are at a standoff with each other.

Some may argue that the "just do it" strategy sweeps important stuff under the rug or uses sex as a cure-all. I disagree. In fact, in some cases, too much talk and too little physical contact can land you in divorce court. You need a way to rebooting your sex life. So why not give "just do it" a try? Close your mouths, open your arms, jump into the abyss of sex, and see what happens.

It is common for couples in recovery to avoid openly facing the state of their sex life when things are going bad. Instead of dealing with sexual problems, the codependent may relapse into old controlling and caretaking tactics. Although solidly in second stage recovery, the addict may head for relapse to avoid feelings of shame, helplessness, anger, and frustration. This is usually when you are most likely to separate or divorce prematurely. So don't hesitate to seek outside help if you are stuck in a sexless or no-desire cycle with your recovering partner. Therapy can interrupt that cycle or shorten its duration.

TRY THIS: Mindfully Light Up Your Sexuality

This kundalini yoga technique, called Breath of Fire, not only energizes your body and your mind, but also calms your nervous system and reconnects you to your whole body. It can help you jump-start your sex drive. This is also an amazing exercise to do when you are feeling anxious, fearful, depressed, or trapped in a mental state you want to get out of. If you need a visual aid to understand how to do Breath of Fire, go to YouTube.com and search for "Breath of Fire." You will find many different variations.

You can do Breath of Fire alone or with your partner.

1. Sit up straight, either in a chair or cross-legged on the floor. Place your right hand on your abdomen so that you can feel your stomach move as you breathe. When you inhale through your nose, your stomach goes out. When you exhale through your nose, your stomach goes in.

2. Equalize the length of your inhale and exhale. If you put your fingers in your ears, you can hear your breath going in and out in equal amounts.

3. Now forcibly exhale through your nose, using your abdominal muscles to force the air out. With your hand, feel your stomach pull inward. You will hear a sound as you exhale.

4. Repeat the above steps for nine complete breaths at a time—this is one round. Do three rounds of this to complete the exercise. Do not pause between breaths or between rounds. As you become more practiced, you may choose to add more rounds.

Contraindications for this exercise for women include being pregnant or being in the first two days of your menstrual cycle. For those of you who would otherwise rather not do this exercise, you can get a jump rope and jump for three minutes straight and it will produce much the same result. You will be energized; activate your sexuality; and, well, basically just come alive!

Tackle Your Fear of Intimacy

Another factor that can dampen your sexual desire is fear of being intimate. Like George and Kathy, you may never have felt truly connected to your partner without his or her addiction being involved. Codependents are prone to avoiding their true emotions and instead wrongly equate high emotionality with being intimate. It can be hard to tolerate the anxious feelings of vulnerability, awkwardness, and self-consciousness that accompany true intimacy.

Achieving an honest, intimate connection always involves at least some of those feelings. Why? Because intimacy means exposing what is personal and private for you. To find connection, you must risk disappointment, rejection, misunderstanding, or even disgust from your partner. Sexual intimacy requires you to ride the waves of discomfort while at the same time remaining in contact with your partner. This is not an easy feat for anyone, much less a codependent and the partner he or she loves. Nevertheless, allowing yourself to be known by your partner at a deeper level can bring about profound connection. I encourage you to let yourself feel uncomfortable, nervous, embarrassed, or awkward—whatever it takes to bring more intimacy into your relationship. By the way, this also builds nerves of steel!

Of course, you shouldn't always rely on sex to bring you together. Intimacy begins way before you get into the bedroom. You want to be able to soothe each other's hurts and repair any wounds, as well as to turn each other on sexually. Being flirtatious, adding an erotic touch to your good-bye kiss in the morning, and sending loving texts throughout the day may send shivers up your partner's spine, and help you and your recovering partner get back into the sexual flow. Here are some other actions that can serve as foreplay to increase intimacy and ultimately lead to sex:

- Take a long, hot shower together.

- Read poetry together.

- Dance in the kitchen.

- Sit across from each other and gaze into each other's eyes without speaking.

- Take a walk around the block while holding hands.

We know from the work of Cindy Hazan and Phillip Shaver, as well as other attachment theorists, that adult partners need plenty of holding and hugging to maintain their bond with each other in much the same way that a baby needs to be held by its parents to form a healthy bond with them. If a baby does not get many daily doses of connection and cuddling, distress and anxiety may result. If this happens too often and for too long, the baby is likely to grow up without the ability to form secure connections with others. These fundamental principles of attachment theory apply to you and your partner. You too need consistent and predictable exchanges of love and affection to feel close, safe, and trusting. The following exercise may seem a little strange at first, but if you can get past feeling self-conscious, it will help you and your recovering partner soothe each other. Holding each other in this way will increase your connection, help you feel safer with each other, and maybe also stimulate sexual desire.

TRY THIS: The Mindful Sleigh Ride

Find a comfortable space on the floor or on your bed. Sit with your back against the wall and your arms wrapped around your partner, while your partner sits between your legs with his or her back against you. Or vice versa. Think of how you would ride on a sled or motorcycle together. Without facing each other, you will be creating connection.

1. Sit like this for seven minutes. Don't talk—just breathe.

2. Close your eyes and synchronize your breathing.

3. Notice how long it takes for you to feel relaxed and calm together.

4. If you aren't able to achieve your most relaxed state, don't worry; you will if you practice this often.

5. At the end of the exercise, take note of how you're feeling with your partner. Do you feel closer? More distant? The same?

The Power of the Past

You may be thinking, "Beverly, is there no end to the issues that come up in recovery?" The answer is, "Nope." This chapter would not be complete without addressing how your level of desire can be affected by what you bring to the relationship. This includes sexual trauma and infidelity, either by your partner or on your part. Neither sexual trauma nor infidelity was an issue George and Kathy had to deal with in their relationship. But this is not the case for many couples in recovery, so I include these issues here.

Sexual Trauma

One of the most profound roadblocks to developing a robust sexuality is having been physically or sexually abused. Sexual trauma is disturbingly prevalent in our society, and it runs the gamut from subtle incestuous innuendo, to inappropriate touching, naked exposure, sexual stimulation, oral sex, and full penetration and forceful rape. Although many think only girls are victims of sexual abuse, this is not true. Many boys are subjected to these experiences by parents, neighbors, relatives, or strangers.

Sexual abuse, child abuse, and molestation are terrible experiences that can have devastating effects on the normal development of a person's sexuality. A child's position of vulnerability in relation to a powerful figure who dominates and exploits him or her sexually creates fear, self-hatred, and a deep mistrust of others. It is not uncommon for codependents and their recovering partners to carry sexual trauma that stays hidden until recovery brings their pain to the surface. If sexual trauma is in your history, your sex life will be more difficult to sort out than that of someone who has not had this happen.

Issues of sexual abuse are best treated by a professional, who can create a safe atmosphere to heal sexual wounds. As difficult as it might be, it is best for you and your recovering partner to tell each other if either of you have abuse in your history. There is a saying in Alcoholics Anonymous: "You're only as sick as your secrets." So you don't want to have shame or guilt hold you hostage because you are keeping your past a secret from the most important people in your life. Especially your recovering partner!

Infidelity, Intrigue, and Betrayal

In today's world of technology, our notion of what constitutes a transgression in relationships has expanded greatly. With the advent of online pornography, chat rooms, instant messaging, and Facebook, couples can be hard pressed to clearly define their guidelines for loyalty, trust, and safety and what they consider cheating.

So how do you know when you or your partner has crossed a line? The truth is, you cross a line as soon as you break any explicit agreement you and your partner have made. Perhaps you discussed monogamy before you even slept together. Or maybe you had a "don't ask, don't tell" policy in effect until you declared a commitment to each other. Some couples have open marriages, or open relationships, but that is not the norm. Whether explicitly expressed or not, most people expect their partner to remain emotionally and physically faithful and build trust on that expectation. If you and your partner have defined the rules of being faithful and what constitutes cheating, as soon as either of you violates them, the emotional outcome is the same: deep feelings of betrayal, rejection, and mistrust.

The shock of discovering an affair often leads to depression, anger, shame, obsessive thoughts, inability to concentrate, and hypervigilant monitoring of a partner's every move. Someone whose partner has cheated on him or her can be left with shattered feelings and trauma similar to that of an abused child. Although the adult is, of course, less helpless in such a situation, the resulting hurt can still be profoundly disturbing.

If your partner cheated on you, he or she may not have insight into why. Or he or she may not be ready to openly discuss the details of the affair and what motivated it. Regardless, you may need the whole truth about an affair revealed to you so that you can heal and rebuild trust, even if it is difficult and causes great pain in the relationship. Or you may not want to know any of the details. Either way, you will most likely need your partner to sincerely apologize, to show empathy for your position, and to be willing to patiently soothe you in ways that work for you. The same thing goes for you if you were the one who betrayed the relationship.

It may be possible to wend your way back to a trusting place, and sometimes to an even more intimate one, after you've overcome betrayal. In other words, if you put in enough effort, past infidelities can really be a thing of the past. They do not have to destroy your relationship. Overcoming the injury caused by betrayal is a process that requires patience. It takes time to rebuild trust. So don't be in too much of a rush.

TRY THIS: Mindfully Exploring Past Infidelity, Intrigues, and Betrayals

If your recovering partner was unfaithful during his or her days of addiction, be rigorously honest and mindfully ask yourself the following questions:

- *Do I believe in my heart that my partner is sorry for betraying me?*

- *Do I think my recovering partner is still justified in defending his or her past behavior?*

- *Do I believe that now that my partner is in recovery he or she can be trusted to be honest and stay within the guidelines we set up together?*

- *Do I feel my recovering partner is being falsely compliant out of fear or is sincere in his or her efforts to heal our relationship?*

- *Can I forgive myself for staying with my recovering partner even though he or she hurt me?*

- *Do I fear I'm always going to kick myself for staying with my partner after he or she cheated on me?*

- *Do I believe my partner is on a recovering path and wants to grow?*

- *Do I believe my partner can forgive himself or herself?*

- *Do I believe I can forgive my partner?*

If you were the partner who was unfaithful, mindfully ask yourself the following questions:

- *Am I truly sorry for betraying my partner?*

- *Do I still feel I had good reason to justify my cheating?*

- *Do I believe I can be trusted to stay within the guidelines we set up together?*

- *Am I being falsely compliant out of fear, or am I being sincere in my efforts to heal past hurts in my relationship?*

- *Do I believe my partner really forgives me for breaking the trust in our relationship and hurting him or her?*

- *Do I fear my recovering partner will always be angry with himself or herself for having stayed with me?*

- *Do I believe I am on a path of recovery and want to grow?*

- *Can I forgive myself?*

- *Can I forgive my partner?*

Regardless of your answers, if you can be honest with yourself and start exploring exactly how you feel and where you are coming from, you can begin to move from deep mistrust back to trust. These answers are meant to give you a sense of where to begin a conversation with your partner, not to predict where you might end up.

When the most pressing hurts and past injuries have been addressed, you will have a better understanding of what you need in order to have a truly trustworthy and nourishing sex life with your recovering partner. While working through the shame and pain of past hurts or betrayals, make sure you have the phone numbers of a few good therapists who specialize in trauma and couples therapy to turn to if the volume on the pain and stress gets too high.

Conclusion

This chapter has suggested ways to beef up your autonomy, make claims on your sexuality, connect with your partner through physical contact and open communication, and heal betrayal in order to have regular, and even good, sex again. Don't be discouraged if your efforts are clumsy and downright ineffective some of the time. Navigating sex, avoiding reactivity, and trusting that your sex life can get better may take every ounce of blind faith you can muster. Remember to rely on your mindful meditation practice to find your center, and observe your process as you investigate your sex life. So, hang tight. As long as you're willing to try a little bit each day, you will see incremental results toward a sensual, erotic, connected, playful, and varied sex life that may surpass anything you've had with your recovering partner before.

CHAPTER 7

Exploring Spirituality: What's God Got to Do with It?

Addiction is a master at destroying spirit and faith whenever it crosses anyone's path. That includes the path of the codependent. Addiction and codependency are spiritual maladies: the addict uses addiction to fill the hole in his or her soul, and the codependent uses the addict to fill the hole in his or her soul. Recovery offers the chance for both to restore their lost faith. Millions of recovering people attest to spiritual practice as a great source of hope, strength, comfort, and peace. This is why it is essential to identify what spirituality means to you.

This chapter will show you how to discover a spiritual life you may not yet know, or how to incorporate your current spiritual life into your recovery. It will also shed light on the role spirituality can play in your recovery from codependency and in your relationship with your recovering partner. Just as you investigated where your frame of reference for relationship came from in chapter 1, you will discover your frame of reference for spirituality in this chapter.

Discovering Spirituality

The word *spirit* means different things to different people. Spirit comes from the Latin *spiritus*, meaning "breath," so one meaning is that with every breath you take, your spirit breathes life into your soul. Living a spiritual life in this sense might simply be about breathing life into your essential nature, or spirit, where your truest desires, intuition, and highest intelligence live within you. Another view of spirit is as the life force that is both inside you and all around you and that is the ruling power of the universe.

Similarly, you may equate *spirituality* with nature, energy, or the natural flow of life. Or you may think of it as whatever brings a sense of awe and wonderment and innocence to your life. Perhaps spirituality is what oxygenates your faith when fear, anxiety, and negative thinking are taking up too much space in your head and heart. You don't need to start wearing white robes or putting a string around your wrist or saying "*Om*" to be spiritual. You can if you want to; you just don't have to.

Much as science is dedicated to exploration of the external world, spirituality is dedicated to exploration of our inner world. Scientists have not been able to quantify or prove the existence of God, though some continue to try. In the meantime, the mysteries of life can be placed in the realm of God, religion, and spirituality.

Unlike science and religion, spirituality does not have strict rules or restrictions. It is not organized around a particular dogma. For this reason, you may be more comfortable being involved with a spiritual life than a religious one. In essence, spirituality refers to any relationship you have with something that lies beyond the physical, psychological, and social dimensions of life. You might call that God or awareness of a higher power. You can connect to it through mindfulness meditation, contemplation, or prayer, or simply taking a walk in nature. Sometimes all it takes is looking up at the sun, or at the moon and stars, to get immediate evidence the universe has elements within it that are much bigger than our small bodies and holds answers we have yet to discover.

"Contempt prior to investigation" is a phrase frequently used in 12-step programs to refer to our tendency to have preconceived notions that render us unwilling to consider new ideas. Saying no to spirituality before attempting to discover what you're saying no to will not serve you. Many people spend a lifetime seeking answers to questions about the mysteries of the universe, including God and spirituality. You are free to take as long as you need to investigate the subject in any way you wish. It's a pretty big subject, so be prepared to spend some time thinking before you reach any final conclusions.

Question: "Why Are People Telling Me I Need to Have a Spiritual Practice to Improve My Relationship, When I'm Not Religious and Don't Believe in God?"

Leslie and Owen were in their early forties, had been married for twelve years, and had two children. Leslie had threatened to leave Owen multiple times because of the hours he spent online having cybersex and combing through social networks. Each time she caught him, Owen begged her to stay, and she always conceded to his convincing promises that he would stop. Things came to a head when Leslie found a credit card bill in Owen's name for an account she was unaware existed. The bill was more than $6,000 for online sex sites

Owen had visited. This was the last straw. Leslie went to a divorce attorney and presented Owen with divorce papers. At that point, Owen decided to enter a twenty-eight-day treatment program for sex addiction. His aftercare included attending Sex Addicts Anonymous meetings and seeing an addiction specialist for recovery from sexual addiction.

Leslie had a long history of being attracted to and getting involved with addicts. Although her relationships always ended painfully, she found it nearly impossible to resist the excitement of an addictive personality. Leslie did not grow up in a household where either parent was an addict, but her grandfather on her mother's side was an active alcoholic until the day he died. Owen grew up with an alcoholic father and swore to himself he would never become like his father. As Leslie's grandmother had done, Owen's mother stayed with her husband until he died. Once again, I am reminded of how often addiction is rooted in the family tree, and how the unconscious pull of codependents toward addicts passes from generation to generation until the chain is broken by recovery.

When I met this couple, Owen had abstained from all cybersex activities for ten months, as well as from surfing the web in general. He had not relapsed, was actively working the 12 steps, and had daily contact with a sponsor. But even so, Leslie could not stop obsessing about his every move, and felt resentful much of the time. She had let her life go by while waiting for Owen to get into recovery, and now she was letting her life go by waiting for him to make convincing amends for all the pain he had caused her with his addictive behavior. She had lost faith in Owen, herself, and their relationship, and this loss left her in a state of anger, despair, sadness, and isolation. Nevertheless, her willingness to go with Owen to a therapist showed that she still hoped to avoid that final heartbreaking decision.

During our first meeting, I asked Leslie about the role that God or spirituality played in her life. This stopped the conversation cold.

She said, "God? I don't believe in God. This is the problem I am having with those Al-Anon meetings. Everyone talks about God, and I don't want to talk about God. They say I can find my higher power in the rooms of Al-Anon, but I know that's not true. They want me to believe in God, and they're just trying to sneak it in through the back door. I don't believe in God, and I never will. So don't get started on this spirituality stuff!"

I told her that in spite of her feelings, if she was serious about seeing what might make her relationship work, she'd be wise to add investigating the subject of spirituality into the mix.

She quickly responded with, "Why are people telling me I need to have a spiritual practice to improve my relationship, when I'm not religious and don't believe in God?"

Like Leslie, you may have a knee-jerk reaction against spirituality. For example, you may harbor sad or painful memories related to encounters with religion during childhood. As a result, the mere thought of God or a higher power may leave a bad taste in your mouth. Or, as an adult, you may have seen all the pain and suffering people cause each other in the name of religious doctrine, and want no part of it. All I am suggesting is that for right now you make a decision to mindfully set your negative preconceived notions of spirituality aside so that you can be open to new experiences as part of your recovery.

You never know what might happen, or when, if you open your mind to a new curiosity about spirituality. You could be going for an early morning hike, watching the most glorious sunrise, with the birds chirping and the wind blowing, and suddenly your heart feels wide open and you think, *Wow! What a magical moment! Maybe this is what people mean when they say their higher power lives in their heart and connects them to the beauty of the world around them.* In that moment, you experience a sense of what could be called a higher power. It's not just a concept someone was trying to make you believe in while you were growing up. The experience of that sunrise stays with you as an internal reference point that you can turn to, trust, and connect with, and that you may choose to call your higher power.

If you live mindfully, you will begin to notice so many simple but ecstatic and beautiful moments in your daily life that give you a feeling of faith. I encourage you to take refuge in these moments and to draw upon them when needed to fuel serenity and to connect deeply with yourself. These are the moments you can define as your connection with a higher power. Some of these experiences happen randomly, and others are brought about by mindful actions you take. These actions add up to what you can call your spiritual practice in recovery.

No God, No Higher Power, No Spirituality

You may be the type of recovering codependent who says, "I am an atheist" or "I am an agnostic" and wonder, "Where do I fit in?" If you are an atheist or an agnostic, the kind of spirituality I am talking about simply means becoming mindful of the actions that fuel your faith in the sustainability of your relationship and enable you to cope with whatever life hands you. You don't have to follow a religious or spiritual path to listen to the sounds around you or even to benefit from listening to great sermons. You can do these things without ever uttering the words "God" or "higher power."

For the record, no one path works for everybody, but every path works for someone. If going to museums and viewing exquisite art helps you connect with the best of yourself and brings you a feeling of love toward your recovering partner, then let that be your spirituality. If music makes your soul sing and opens your heart to have more generosity toward your partner, then let music be your religion. Whatever it is, if it brings back connection to your relationship and helps you transcend your fears, anxieties, and unending hungers, then stick with it and call it your higher power. There is no need to become dogmatic about the right and wrong paths for people to follow. What's important is that you find the right actions and practices in your own daily life that bring about the kinds of results that other people get from what they call their spiritual path. I asked Leslie if she was at least willing to contemplate spirituality, and she agreed to do the following exercise.

TRY THIS: Mindfully Awaken the Spirit That Resides in You

As you contemplate these questions about spirituality, be mindful of the thoughts, sensations, and emotions you experience. Remember, don't judge what comes up for you; just take note of it. Feel free to write your answers in a journal. You may want to look at them a year from now.

1. What have you turned to when you felt disillusioned with life?

2. If you could define a higher power that fits you well, how would you define it?

3. What does spirituality mean to you?

4. Are there any spiritual people you admire and want to emulate? Who are they, and why them?

5. Do you believe change is possible through prayer and meditation?

6. Have you had experiences with prayer and meditation that strengthened your faith in a higher power?

7. Are you willing to incorporate a daily spiritual practice into your life? With your recovering partner?

8. What do you fear about spirituality?

9. What do you trust about spirituality?

10. What did your parents teach you about religion, prayer, or spirituality, and how do you think that influences your views today?

There are no right answers to these questions, of course. All I'm asking is that you be willing to explore spirituality from every angle and allow yourself the opportunity to come up with some new and different ideas, or to confirm the ones you already hold dear. Again, as with any exercise you do in this book, be gentle and compassionate toward yourself, and take all judgment off the table. At this point on your journey, your answers can put you back in control of sculpting what you want to call your higher power and discovering the actions that will make up your spiritual future.

The Dark Night of the Soul

Like Leslie, you may be struggling to feel hopeful about your relationship, even with recovery in the mix. If you can focus more on discovering or rediscovering your faith in life and focus less on your relationship with your recovering partner, you will start to feel a stronger sense of control and a deeper level of security within yourself. This is one of the keys to your recovery from codependency. Believe it or not, vast growth can occur during times of lost faith. Your perseverance and patience are important at these times because great light, insight, and wisdom can come out of dark periods if you go within and find where faith lives in your heart.

Grief and Loss

Grieving over lost time and lost innocence is an integral part of the recovering codependent's experience. You may be grieving for time you spent trying to make your recovering partner change, only to be betrayed yet again. You may grieve for the loss of the security and trust that your partner's addiction has shattered. Or you may grieve over the time that was lost while you built a world around daily anxieties instead of daily delights.

Real life presents many difficult situations. Grief and loss are as much a part of life as are joy and gain. Having a spiritual practice will not lift you out of real life, nor will it guarantee that you never have to confront hard times again. Your spiritual life should help you cope and thrive, and it should bring mindful awareness and understanding to what you had to bear while you were lost in codependency and your partner was active in addiction, as well as those your experiences now that he or she is in recovery.

Unmetabolized grief can leave you susceptible to bouts of self-criticalness and self-judgment, and unable to let go of the past. For this reason, it is beneficial to find a life-affirming philosophy. Life can feel hard to bear if you think that all the years you spent trying to keep your relationship strong through the trials of your partner's addiction were wasted. It is good to invest time and energy in any philosophy that widens your perspective and allows you to gain wisdom from the hurt and betrayal that addiction inflicted. Whichever philosophy you turn to, make sure it helps you see the narrative of your life as one of survival, strength, wisdom, and compassion, and does not contribute to further self-blame and self-rejection, senseless victimization, or the waste of precious time.

TRY THIS: A Mindful Morning Reading

Whether you are starting from blind faith or borrowed faith, renewed faith or lost faith, having a daily ritual that centers and grounds you is important. You can develop a well-defined spiritual life simply by orienting your mind in the right direction. Therefore, I suggest you begin each day by reaching for your morning reading.

Choose something that is oriented toward any of the following states of mind: peace, calm, collaboration, friendship, or compassion. One passage I like in AA's *The Big Book* (2013) readers gives step-by-step instructions for maintaining serenity and well-being from the moment they wake up until they go to bed at night. You can find it online on pages 86 through 88 of chapter 6. If that passage doesn't speak to you, do an online search for "daily meditations for recovery." You'll find hundreds of offerings to choose from. Many other books have daily contemplations in them, as well, such as *Daily Reflections: A Book of Reflections by A.A. Members for A.A. Members* (1990), *A Day at a Time: Daily Reflections for Recovering People* (1989), and *Courage to Change: One Day at a Time in Al-Anon* (1992). The list is infinite. Even if all you do is read a poem that is inspirational to you, you will be on the right track.

Once you find a reading that works for you, commit to reading it for thirty days straight. (Yes, this is another of those thirty-day things.)

Your recovering partner can share the ritual if he or she chooses. If not, lovingly do it for yourself. If you do this for thirty days and your partner is still wary of your practice, I give you permission to take the reins and tell your partner you are going to read out loud to him or her. Many couples have benefited from doing this in spite of one partner thinking it is cornball or woo-woo. Don't be put off by any cynicism or judgment of your efforts to bring poetry or beautiful writings into both of your lives. Be brave and ignore any disdain or eye rolling. Remember, you are fighting for your autonomy and not looking for approval anymore. You stopped doing that after investigating your sexuality in chapter 6, right? At this point, it is more important to stand by your commitment to making new efforts than it is to strive for your partner's approval.

Watch what this daily ritual does to transform your relationship. It's not a somber activity. You can have fun while you do it. While I make no promises, bringing good words into your home can help you pull the plug on your fear, self-will, and anxiety, and it may even be one of the most significant actions you take to save your relationship from being hijacked by negative thinking each day.

TRY THIS: Action-Oriented Spiritual Practice

If you select a daily practice that inspires and supports your efforts to have faith in your relationship, whether you realize it or not, you will be living a spiritual life. Collaboration, being of service, self-love, and compassion are essential ingredients of spirituality. Even if your choices are not exactly the same as those of your partner, what matters is that you have respect for each other's brand of spirituality.

The following is a list of mindful actions you can take to support your recovery. Some of these activities can be done on a daily or regular basis; others are occasional practices. Feel free to create a list of your own.

1. Spend time in nature.

2. Pray.

3. Meditate.

4. Be of service in your community to those less fortunate.

5. Go on a retreat.

6. Listen to your favorite music and sing out loud while dancing in your living room.

7. Write a gratitude list.

8. Tell your recovering partner that you love him or her unconditionally.

9. Write a thank-you note to someone who has made a difference in your life.

10. Give your old clothes to a homeless shelter.

11. Become a big brother or a big sister.

12. Pray for someone toward whom you hold resentment.

13. Apologize to someone to whom you were insensitive.

14. Talk to someone about his or her problems; offer your experience, strength, and hope.

15. Take a yoga class.

16. Chant.

17. Introduce two people you love to each other.

18. Donate to a charity you believe in.

19. Lend a hand where you can.

20. Hold a baby in your arms and sing him or her a lullaby.

Question: "I Don't Know How to Pray or Meditate. Isn't There an Easier Way?"

Leslie was willing to contemplate spirituality, and she reported at our next meeting that she was able to define a spirituality for herself that was distinct from her prior negative associations with religion. She enjoyed doing the mindful morning reading ritual with Owen, and when I suggested that she find an action-oriented spiritual practice, she quickly selected a community service project.

I was glad to see Leslie had found a new definition and a comfort zone with her spirituality, but I also sensed she was limiting herself by exploring only spiritual practices she was comfortable with already. So I asked her if she ever meditated.

Leslie made a face. "That hippy-dippy nonsense? Meditation is not the answer here. Owen staying clean, away from the Internet, and trying to be more considerate of me is. Besides, I don't know how to pray or meditate. Isn't there an easier way?"

I explained to Leslie what I consider to be the value of prayer and meditation. These practices are tried and true ways to let anxiety and fear fall away and to drop into a peaceful sense of security. Not only have they been practiced for centuries in many parts of the world, but recent research (like Carter, 1998) has also demonstrated their effectiveness for individuals in recovery. Meditation helps you become more mindful of yourself through self-observation and less likely to react negatively to your recovering partner. It brings awareness into the present and makes living more mindful and less automatic. Prayer, on the other hand, actively directs the mind toward goodwill to others and yourself.

Most codependents wake up each day with fearful, hungry egos that mess with their serenity. Remember Audrey II, the man-eating plant from the 1986 movie *Little Shop of Horrors*? If not, I will remind you: She had to be fed every day, but no matter how much she consumed, she wanted more and more. Well, that is how your hungry ego operates. If you feed it, it always wants more. It will do its best to convince you to grab as much as you can, not just from your recovering partner, but also from the entire world around you. It will never be satisfied, and it certainly isn't asking what it can do to be of service to others. The ego is interested in surviving other egos, not being in community with them.

Meditation is one of the most effective ways I know to get out from underneath your ego's endless wants and needs, and back to a place within yourself where you feel satisfied and grateful for what you have. To recover from anxiety and negative thinking, you may have to remind yourself many times throughout the day to calm down, take a breath, turn toward yourself, observe, and listen to what your mind is saying. Luckily for you, you've been doing mindful meditation throughout this book already and are probably getting somewhat acquainted with its benefits.

"Okay, maybe meditation works," Leslie said. "But I don't hear you saying anything about it being easy."

I said, "You can end up going around in circles trying to find an easier, softer way in recovery. But if you want different results in your relationship, you need to try some things you don't feel like trying. And that may feel difficult."

Meditation is one of those things. Saying "yes!" is your way of fighting against contempt prior to investigation. You can start to build a spiritual life in as little as three minutes in the morning and three minutes at night. All you have to do is meditate for ninety seconds and read a small prayer or spiritual reading out loud for ninety seconds. Ninety seconds! Just that small gesture can make the difference between creating well-being in your home and running on tension from the moment the alarm clock goes off.

When I put it that way, Leslie had to agree that ninety seconds was not a lot to ask. In fact, it might turn out to be easy after all.

Practice Meditation

Within one month, Leslie reported feeling the positive effects of prayer and meditation. She felt less angry and more able to express her sad feelings, and her heart felt more open toward Owen. I explained to her that meditation increases alpha waves in the brain, which would account for her increased feelings of well-being. I can pretty much guarantee that you, like Leslie, will reap the benefits of mindful meditation even if you only practice for a short time each day. Again, these practices haven't been around for thousands of years for no reason.

MINDFULNESS MEDITATION: Connect with Faith

Read these instructions to yourself, then put down the book and do the meditation.

1. Close your eyes. Take a deep breath in and a long, slow breath out, and allow yourself to relax. Notice where you are holding tension in your body. Breathe into those places and allow yourself to relax more fully.

2. As you continue breathing, allow yourself to notice any sensations that arise in your body.

3. Ask yourself, "How would I feel if I could trust in a power greater than myself?"

4. Next ask yourself, "If I could have any kind of spiritual life with my recovering partner, what would it be like?" Notice what sensations, thoughts, emotions, and images arise as you ponder this question.

5. As you continue to relax, let each breath take you deeper into a state of curiosity about the future of your spiritual life. Breathe in the possibility of what you would like in your spiritual life. Breathe out any resistance you have to your spiritual life being exactly as it is at this moment.

6. Whenever you feel ready, open your eyes.

Practice Prayer

Depending on their beliefs, people position themselves for prayer by sitting, kneeling, lying on the floor, folding their hands, bowing their head, or looking to the skies above. You can pray out loud or in your mind. You can recite prayers you know, read them from a book, or make them up yourself. Whichever way you like best, prayer is a door you go through in your mind to commune with your higher power, God, or your own truest self.

Those who pray regularly say it opens a channel to let love in and let hate out. Prayer is not a selfish, self-serving act. It is an opportunity to be of service just by asking what you can do for others, rather than what they can do for you. You can pray for inspiration, higher awareness, or gratitude; you can pray to be relieved of fear or to be shown what your true purpose is in life. There is no need to wait until a crisis occurs in your life to pray. Make prayer part of your daily life, just like brushing your teeth.

TRY THIS: Show Me My Higher Power

If you haven't prayed before, try this. Sit with your hands in your lap, close your eyes, and say this little prayer to yourself: "I don't know, but I'm willing to know. If there is such a thing as a higher power, thank you for showing me what it is now. Show me, show me, show me."

Repeat this to yourself every morning when you wake up and each night before you go to sleep.

Reciting this prayer is an act of humility. It starts with your willingness to not know how to pray, and your willingness to spend a little time each day practicing it anyway. The key to prayer is directing your thinking. It is as simple as that.

TRY THIS: A Mindful Letter to God

Now, even if you don't believe it, imagine that God, or a higher power, does exist. Sit down and mindfully write a letter to this God. Ask any questions of God that you would like to ask. Say anything to God that you would like to say. Don't hold back. If you are mad at God, let God know this. If you don't believe in the existence of God, let God know that, too.

Notice what feelings, thoughts, and sensations come up as you do this. Ask yourself, "How old do I feel right now as I write my letter to God?" Let yourself know the answer to that question.

So Many Paths, So Little Time...

Being on a spiritual path on which you and your recovering partner learn how to grow out of self-centered fear and into expansive faith is essential to ensuring future love between you. Again, you don't need to kneel at altars, become religious, or wear spiritual robes to succeed at this. You should do these things if your heart is calling you to do them, but you don't have to. What I am suggesting has to do with cultivating a state of mind that inspires self-love and sympathy for your partner, and that shows you how to creatively engage with your pain so that greater understanding and inspiration can come of it.

You may be wondering if, to survive and thrive with your partner, you must go to 12-step meetings. The truth is, I'm not sure about that. In the thirty years I've worked in recovery I haven't met many addicts, or partners of addicts, who really enjoy their partnership without having found their way on a devotional path of some kind. The majority of these people go to a 12-step program and have lots of friends who go, as well. They may wander off and find a Buddhist meditation center, synagogue, church, or other spiritual path, but the 12-step program remains their foundation. Nowadays you can find some kind of 12-step meeting practically every day, in every city or state, with meetings at morning, noon, and night.

As you deepen your spiritual path in recovery with your partner, you will both work to give more to each other and take less. If you don't do this, you can count on your hungry ego running the show. A daily practice will slowly dissolve egoistic thinking and encourage an attitude toward your partner that is based on kindness, compassion, love, and respect. After a while, your daily practice will bring about the realization that you and your partner are good people who struggle with addiction and codependency and not bad people trying to be good.

TRY THIS: Twelve Indicators You Have a Spiritual Practice

The following statements are guideposts to give you a sense of what you can gain or have gained from following a regular spiritual practice. I'm sure these are not the only indicators, but they are the fundamental ones you can count on. It's always good to have reference points that distinguish between a life based on faith and a life run by fear.

1. I have an increased ability to let things happen rather than try to make them happen.

   TRUE   FALSE

2. I know I'm going to be okay, no matter what my condition is.

   TRUE   FALSE

3. I feel connected with others and with nature much of the time.

   TRUE   FALSE

4. I have frequent episodes of overwhelming appreciation and gratitude for what I have.

   TRUE   FALSE

5. I have an increased tendency to think clearly, act spontaneously, and enjoy each moment.

   TRUE   FALSE

6. I have lost my tendency to worry constantly.

   TRUE   FALSE

7. I have lost interest in unnecessary conflict with my recovering partner.

   TRUE   FALSE

8. I have lost interest in judging my recovering partner.

   TRUE   FALSE

9. I have lost interest in judging myself.

   TRUE   FALSE

10. I have gained the ability to love my recovering partner without expecting anything in return.

    TRUE   FALSE

11. I do mindful meditation.

    TRUE   FALSE

12. I pray regularly.

    TRUE   FALSE

If you are reading this chapter for the first time and just beginning to explore spirituality in the context of your recovery, you may not yet rate most of these statements as true for yourself. In that case, I suggest you review these statements again in a month or two. When more than half are true for you, you can feel confident you have found a spiritual practice that works for you. That percentage should keep increasing the longer you practice.

Spiritual Bypass

You may already have a strong spiritual practice and trust in a higher power with which you feel secure 99 percent of the time. If so, fantastic! I hope this chapter affirms what you already know to be true. But if you are sustaining a daily spiritual practice and are still lacking connection in your relationship, the problem may be that you are using your spirituality to forgive prematurely, to avoid the pain of unresolved trauma, or to stay in a dissociated state of starry-eyed religiosity.

The term *spiritual bypass* refers to the tendency to hide out in prayer and meditation to avoid dealing with emotions and the hard edges of life. This is not meant to be an indictment of your spiritual practice. However, you may be using it counterproductively. Your spiritual practice is there to support you, not to numb you out or to keep you from being more connected to your sadness or grief. If you are using it in this way, try to identify the feelings you need to face. You can use prayer to give you the strength to hold up under the weight of your emotions and to let yourself experience your emotions fully.

Conclusion

At the end of the day, to find lasting happiness, you must take the act of committing to a daily practice seriously. This can make the difference between a day of joyful celebration, serenity, and connection and a day of anxious worry, agitation, and disconnection. Don't be discouraged if your effort to build your spiritual life doesn't bring about a huge change in your relationship right away. It is more about experimenting, never giving up, and self-discipline. Treat your practice as something that gets richer and reaps fuller benefits over time. Because it will.

You may be on your spiritual quest by yourself right now, and that is fine. In that case, remember to say a little prayer for your recovering partner each day, and don't mention that the walk you are taking in nature with him or her is part of the spiritual path you are exploring in your relationship. Or your recovering partner may be happy to join in prayer and meditation with you. Take your time to explore what you both believe will boost your spiritual connection. What's most important is that your intentions are clear and have been openly negotiated. If both of you can begin exploring the spiritual, no matter what your circumstances are, you will discover a deeper intimacy with yourself and your recovering partner than you ever thought possible.

CHAPTER 8

Settling Down Together: Staying on Track

Throughout this book you've been guided in breaking your fantasy spell, creating boundaries, dealing with moods and emotions, addressing resentments, and keeping your fear low and faith high. I've also offered you ways to improve your communication style and explore your sex life. This chapter will show you that it is possible to attain the gold standard of settling down together and staying in recovery. It will help you address emotional relapse and show you the importance of having a community connection. It will also help you to determine, once and for all, whether the recovering partner with whom you are working to have that gold standard is ultimately the right one for you. Once you know you are in with both feet, you can mindfully create the vows and ethics you want to live by with your recovering partner from that day forward.

Emotional Relapse for the Codependent

Traditionally, the term *relapse* has been associated with the addict. The addict steps off the path of recovery and steps back into addiction as a way to cope with negative mental states, painful emotions, or difficult life situations. Relapse for the codependent occurs when old controlling and self-neglecting behaviors are used to cope with these same types of challenges.

Hopefully, if you find yourself in emotional relapse, your tools of recovery are within arm's reach. If you've ever cooked with an old-fashioned gas stove, you know that it has a pilot light that can go out. You have to keep an eye on that pilot in case it needs to be relit. Similarly, your recovery has its own pilot light. To minimize the damage of emotional relapse, you have to be mindful of whatever might make that light go out, and you have to know how to turn it back on.

You don't have to imagine emotional relapse as a constant threat looming over your head, but you do need to be respectfully aware of its possibility. The more aware you are of the indicators of emotional relapse, the easier it will be for you to identify when you're in it and to get out of it as quickly as possible.

TRY THIS: Common Indicators of Emotional Relapse

Review the following statements and check those with which you identify.

- ☐ I've stopped using my tools of recovery.

- ☐ I am trying to control my recovering partner again.

- ☐ I've entirely stopped feeling gratitude for my recovering partner.

☐ I feel resentment toward my recovering partner brewing beneath the surface.

☐ I've started bad-mouthing my partner behind his or her back.

☐ I've stopped making an effort to go out on dates with my partner.

☐ I've stopped having sex with my recovering partner.

☐ I've stopped hugging my recovering partner hello and good-bye each day.

☐ I've been speaking to my recovering partner in a rude or nasty tone of voice.

☐ I've stopped giving my recovering partner the benefit of the doubt.

☐ I feel indifferent to my recovering partner's suffering.

☐ I break promises I've made to my recovering partner.

☐ I've stopped taking care of myself.

☐ I've lost all interest in doing the things I know make my recovering partner happy.

Review these statements every day for a period of at least two weeks. It's natural to identify with many of these statements from time to time; however, if you find yourself consistently identifying with three or more of these statements, consider yourself in an emotional relapse.

Stressors That Can Blow Out the Pilot Light of Your Recovery

Falling into emotional relapse does not necessarily mean you have been working the wrong program or are in the wrong relationship.

Any time you don't have sufficient support in place to help you cope with the stressors that show up in your life, you remain susceptible to emotional relapse. Regular, everyday inconveniences (for example, excessively long work hours, insufficient sleep, financial worries, health problems, and arguments with children, extended family, or friends) can disrupt your recovery if you are not equipped to deal with them appropriately.

Failing to anticipate a problem that has the potential to hurt your relationship, either because you have not encountered it before or because you underestimate the stress it will cause, can trigger emotional relapse. Emotional relapse can creep up on you if you get complacent about following your daily practice or start telling yourself that codependency is a thing of the past to which you are no longer vulnerable. The fact is that you should *always* be mindfully aware of the impact your surroundings and situations have on you and your recovering relationship. Relapse never has to be a permanent state of being, but you can end up staying in it too long if you don't take the right actions to rescue yourself from it.

Mindfully Breaking Out of Emotional Relapse

If you believe you have fallen into an emotional relapse, you can take specific actions to shift yourself out of that state. Here are several effective strategies.

Perform mindful, positive actions that represent the opposite of what you feel. For example, if you're feeling angry and resentful, stop and pay your recovering partner a compliment. Sometimes acting in this kind of contrary manner can eradicate your negative state. If the action is not something you can do in person, feel free to do it by phone, e-mail, or text. Any motion in a positive direction has the potential to help pull you out of emotional relapse.

If mindful, positive actions toward others aren't working to transform your bad state of mind or negative feelings, try doing something positive for yourself. For example, you might get a massage or spend time with a good friend. Such acts of self-love and self-care can bring you gradually back into a state of emotional balance.

Another strategy to combat emotional relapse is to mindfully reconnect with any recovery support groups you have attended in the past. For example, if you are a member of Al-Anon and have a sponsor, now is the time to get back in touch. The 12-step programs protect against emotional relapse by stressing that you should never isolate yourself for too long by staying away from meetings, other members, or sponsors.

Finally, being of service to others can lift you up and out of yourself and bring feelings of joy, self-esteem, and usefulness. Luckily, you have at your fingertips hundreds of ways to be of service to others. To give just one example, going to a local women's shelter and playing with the children for an hour may have the power to lift you out of an emotional relapse. Emotional relapse has a way of disappearing in the face of the positive feelings that being of service brings.

Question: "Why Is Being Part of a Recovering Community So Important for Our Partnership to Thrive?"

When I met them, Robert and David were in their thirties. They had been together for six years, and David had abstained from gambling and alcohol and regularly attended Gamblers Anonymous and Alcoholics Anonymous meetings for three years. His codependent partner, Robert, had not been able to find a Gam-Anon meeting in his area, but he went to Al-Anon meetings on occasion. However, he felt uncomfortable at the meetings and didn't really connect with the other members. He complained that they seemed like a social club of whiners, and he said he found peace more easily by going alone on hikes with their dog.

Both Robert and David had come out to their respective families in high school. Robert was an only child. His parents were very religious and had a strong prejudice against homosexuality. Although they wanted to be tolerant of their son, they found it difficult. After Robert made himself vulnerable to his parents by revealing his sexual orientation, the subject was never brought up again. Their silence made him feel ashamed for many years. Unbeknownst to him, the pain of his parents' silent rejection made it hard for him to feel secure in any group, much less a recovering one.

David's parents reacted to his open expression of homosexuality in the opposite manner. As an expression of advocacy, his mother and father both marched in the Gay Pride Parade one year. Although their love and acceptance did not protect David from drinking excessively and becoming a gambling addict, the comfort of a loving family helped him transition fairly effortlessly into a community of recovering friends and a 12-step program. He felt loved and accepted by his parents, and he expected to be loved and accepted by his new friends in recovery.

David loved Robert very much, but he felt frustrated that Robert refused to be more involved in social activities with other gay couples or events revolving around recovery. He said, "Why can't Robert be more open to enjoying himself with other people who share our experience? I didn't get sober just to isolate us at home." David's individual recovery program had not only given him autonomy, it had highlighted the importance of social interaction. He was ready to take a stand by insisting that Robert value a larger life within community, not just hide on an island with him.

Robert said, "I was happy being single until David came into my life. I don't value being social the way he does and don't feel a strong need to belong to any groups. I can stand by David's side, but why is being part of a recovering community so important for our partnership to thrive?"

Like Robert, you may not understand the importance of being part of a recovering community. Simply put, human beings are social creatures who depend on a sense of belonging and identification with a community to thrive. The root word of "community" is the verb *commune*, which means to come together, to be intimate, to share thoughts and feelings, and to bond with others. As a recovering codependent, you may not realize that you are automatically part of a community of people around the world who are transforming their lives and striving for the same things you are. But you are.

Research by Heller and Swindle (1983) has documented the tremendous positive impact that social support has on well-being, quality of life, longevity, and a sense of belonging. Associating with a community of those in recovery who can understand, sympathize with, and guide you decreases the chances you will relapse emotionally and lose what you've worked so hard to build together. In fact, having the right posse of support to turn to in times of stress is like an insurance policy for your relationship. So I encourage you to consider adding community to your values list, if it isn't there already.

If you, like David, grew up enjoying the company of your family, having lively and interesting family dinners and vacations, and knowing that you could rely on your family for unconditional support, you will be naturally drawn to community involvement or joining groups. You may even feel lost at sea without community involvement. Conversely, if your early family life was fraught with negative feelings, you may be less likely to seek out groups as an adult. Being a part of a group may unconsciously make you feel anxious, uneasy, fearful, or alienated.

In that case, the first step is to understand the value of community so you can mindfully step into a community despite your fears or hesitancy. I believe you can never have too many people to turn to in times of tumult. Programs such as Recovering Couples Anonymous exist solely for the purpose of helping couples follow a path of recovery together. As a recovering codependent once told me, "It was easier for me to make a million dollars than to get along with my partner without the help of my recovering friends!"

Hanging tight with other people who are also in recovery will bring you a sense of community, common purpose, and strength. Group support in an atmosphere of nurturing and unconditional positive regard has the power to heal even the most wounded person. As your new friends walk with you through the process, you can look forward to healing, and your shame and hurt will become a thing of the past. You and your recovering partner need not look too far to find a community of friends who also move in the positive direction you've chosen and who will support you every step of the way.

TRY THIS: Mindfully Create Your Future in Community

Sit down with a cup of tea, and paper and pen, and write down your answers to the following questions. Remember to take a breath, be in the present, and have no judgment about your answers. How you respond today may not be how you will respond tomorrow.

1. With what communities are you and your recovering partner already involved?

2. What positive experiences did you have with these communities before your partner got into recovery?

3. What positive experiences have you had with these communities since your partner got into recovery?

4. How would you describe the community of your family of origin?

5. What problems, if any, do you have being a part of a community as a result of the atmosphere of your family of origin?

6. What assets do you bring to a community as a result of the atmosphere of your family of origin?

7. If you imagine your relationship surrounded by community two years from now, who would be around you?

8. If you imagine your relationship surrounded by community five years from now, who would be around you?

9. What would it take to achieve the community you imagine?

10. What roadblocks would you have to overcome to build community into your life with your recovering partner?

If you still feel uncertain about where you stand on community after answering these questions, don't be concerned. You can feel both uncertain and curious at the same time while you continue to investigate the subject of community.

One way to further explore community is to make a concerted effort to spend time with other couples in recovery. For example, try organizing a dinner for a group of recovering friends with whom you share common interests. You may find that inviting others into your world brings a deeper sense of security to your relationship and enhances your understanding of community.

Question: "In the Long Run, How Do I Know if I'm Really with the Right Partner?"

Although Robert was willing to expand their social involvement to make David happy, he still had fundamental questions about their relationship. He wondered if he and David were truly compatible, given how much effort was required to make their relationship work. He thought it might be easier to be with someone who wasn't an addict in recovery or for whom community involvement was not a value of such importance. Robert couldn't get the nagging question out of his head: "In the long run, how do I know if I'm really with the right partner?"

No one can tell you whether to stay or go, but you can ask yourself some tough questions to clarify your true feelings. What you don't want to do is remain stuck in a state of constant questioning, worry, and fear about being with the wrong person. It is extremely important that you put these concerns to rest so that you can move forward in your recovery.

TRY THIS: Deal Breakers: Should I Stay or Should I Go?

Be honest with yourself as you mindfully review the following deal-breaker questions. Notice the sensations, thoughts, and emotions that arise as you contemplate each.

1. At the bottom of my heart, do I like my recovering partner? (Note that I'm not asking if you *love* your partner.)

2. At the bottom of my heart, do I know that my recovering partner likes me?

3. If I really needed my recovering partner's help in a time of crisis, would he or she be there for me?

4. If my recovering partner really needed my help in a time of crisis, would I be there for him or her?

5. Regardless of how many issues we struggle with, do my recovering partner and I still have activities that we enjoy doing together and that give us a feeling of closeness?

6. Do I know that my recovering partner is basically a good person, even if I feel angry with him or her much of the time?

7. Do I feel confident my recovering partner will treat me in a manner that is free of underlying disrespect, intent to humiliate, or neglect?

8. Do I feel my recovering partner meets a fair share of my needs?

9. Can I say that even if my recovering partner resists addressing certain issues that are important to me, I don't always have to make a big stink to get the attention I want?

10. Can I say that my recovering partner and I have fundamentally similar values, even if we don't give them the same priority?

If you answered no to any of these questions, then it is time to consider ending the relationship. For any relationship to thrive and grow, you must have a fundamental sense that your partner is a good person and that you like and respect each other. It is also imperative that you have ways to come together and feel close and that you value the same basic things in life.

Choosing to Go

If your answers reveal that you should end your relationship, but you don't feel ready to go, now is the time to gather the resources you need to give you the strength to leave. Obviously those resources will be different for everyone. You may be the kind of person who chooses to sit with a wise friend who will hold your hand and help you take the leap. Or you may prefer to take a long walk on a beach alone and let the crashing of the waves empower you. Let yourself turn to whatever you need to support your decision. At the same time, let your recovering partner know you are starting to divest yourself of the relationship, and why. This can sometimes motivate partners to take their relationship more seriously and fight to keep it. You never know.

Making the choice to leave may be one of the hardest things you'll ever have to do, but it probably isn't going to come as a surprise to you, your friends, or your family. Recovery doesn't necessarily keep couples together, but it does bring greater clarity and freedom of choice with respect to the lengths to which you need to go to have happiness in your life.

Choosing to Commit

On the other hand, if your answers reveal confidence about your choice to stay in your relationship with your recovering partner, the next step is to turn and face your future together.

To do this, use the power of conscious intent. What you tell yourself mentally—whether consciously or not—guides your actions, attitude, and feelings. Think of your brain as a good dog that wants to please you. When you tell it what you would like your future with your recovering partner to look like, it hears that not as a suggestion but as a command. Your brain goes, "Okay, my master wants me to fetch appreciation for his or her partner each day. I'm now on alert to notice all the good things my master's recovering partner is doing." This is no joke. Your brain will look for whatever you tell it you want. If you want to move into a full commitment with your recovering partner, I suggest you start to mindfully observe what you are commanding your brain to do for you. Otherwise, it will follow commands you are unaware you are giving.

For example, you may still find yourself frequently thinking, *I'm not sure this is the right relationship for me.* Because you haven't firmly committed to staying, your brain continually offers reasons for leaving. So if you are sincerely committed to staying, send the appropriate command. From this day forward, tell yourself, "I'm here for the long haul. The partner I'm with is the partner I'm choosing. End of story." Giving your brain an unequivocal message will stop you from constantly comparing your partner with others, or questioning whether your partner is right for you. Naturally, these issues may still come up from time to time, but not in a steady stream.

I developed the Mindful Intentions Contract exercise as a way for you to consciously prime your brain to stay focused on your commitment to your partner. By creating such a contract, you agree to leave your past behind. And that includes old frames of reference from your parents' marriage and your childhood. Instead, you commit to starting from scratch, with mindfully intended vows, promises, and aspirations that take both your values and your recovering partner's values into consideration. You can do this exercise with or without your recovering partner's active participation. Why? Because you've decided that your recovering partner is the person you want to be with, and you are going to strive to keep your vows no matter what. Of course, it would be beautiful if your partner were sitting next to you, picking and choosing his or her vows and writing them down, as well. So don't hesitate to ask your partner to do this with you.

All the couples I've used this exercise with over the years have reported it as being hands down the most fun, heartwarming, clarifying, and empowering. So give it all you've got!

TRY THIS: Create a Mindful Intentions Contract

You will need art supplies (construction paper, scissors, glue or tape, stickers, magazines, glitter, markers, crayons, colored pens), plus music you love and can listen to while doing the project.

1. Take a large piece of construction paper and write this heading at the top:

   From this day forward, I (your name) commit to the following intentions:

2. The following statements are examples of what you might want to include in your list. Feel free to make up your own, as well. Mindfully let your imagination flow, and notice the sensations, thoughts, images, and feelings that arise.

- *I intend to hug you daily and surround you with my enduring love.*

- *I intend to treat your love as the most precious gift in my life.*

- *I intend to work mindfully each day so that the love between us will continue to flow.*

- *I intend to take time during the day to remember what I feel grateful for about you, including small things as well as large ones.*

- *I intend to approach our conflicts and difficulties with soundness of mind, and to take responsibility for any dynamics that lead us nowhere.*

- *I intend to practice regulating my own anxiety so that our sex life can be robust, playful, and fulfilling. No matter how long it takes.*

- *I intend to be rigorously honest with myself whenever I harbor upset feelings toward you, and to help us establish a rapport that allows for expression of those feelings.*

- *I intend to be able to say "I'm sorry" sincerely, with no reservation, no defense, and no argument, whenever I have been insensitive or hurtful toward you. Even when I do not understand what I did.*

- *I intend to accept your sincere apologies and forgive you quickly.*

- *I intend to perfect the art of helping you understand the things you do that hurt me, in a way that brings greater intimacy to our relationship.*

- I intend to continue showing you more of who I am and hope to be, so as to bring newness to our relationship.

- I intend to contemplate our relationship and to communicate in ways that truly speak to you.

- I intend to live in the reality of who you are, rather than according to the assumptions my mind creates.

- I intend to let myself be more of who I am, to let you be more of who you are, and to continue challenging myself when I forget to do that.

- I intend to take time each day for prayer and meditation for the well-being of the relationship.

- I intend to keep a sense of humor.

- I intend to remember that you are at the mercy of me.

- I intend to focus on the good of who you are each day.

- I intend to give you the benefit of the doubt no matter how mad you make me.

- I intend to stop assuming so much and to relate more.

- I intend to listen to you carefully.

- I intend to do whatever individual work I need to do to keep our relationship healthy and robust.

- I intend to show you how much I love you in the ways that work best for you, even if these are not the ways that work best for me.

- I intend to stand up for myself and tolerate any conflict that arises.

- I intend to keep working on refining our relationship until we "get it right."

- I intend to know you better and understand you more on a regular basis.

- *I promise to create new promises as we continue to grow and change.*

- *I vow to bring trust to our relationship.*

- *I intend to return to my love for you without condition.*

3. When your list is complete, use your art supplies to decorate the page however you feel best represents your vows.

4. Put your finished contract on a wall where you can see it easily. If your recovering partner is willing to do the same, put his or hers next to yours. Any time you need to reconnect with your vows, take a moment to gaze at your contract. This way, you are reminding your brain of the person you want to be with your recovering partner.

MINDFULNESS MEDITATION:
Consciously Commit to Your Recovering Relationship

Read these instructions to yourself, then put down the book and do the meditation.

1. Take a moment to settle yourself comfortably in a seated position.

2. Close your eyes, or focus on the floor in front of you.

3. Be aware of any tension you might be holding in your body and take as long as you need to let your breath slowly release that tension.

4. Find a place in your body where you can feel a sense of ease and comfort, and put your attention there. Just for now, allow yourself to leave the outside world behind.

5. Take a moment to sink into what it feels like to be fully committed to your recovering partner. Allow yourself to enjoy the prospect of growing closer to your partner. Imagine a future that holds possibilities for your relationship even in the darkest of times. Give yourself permission to feel a sense of safety, confidence, curiosity, and ease. Be proud of who you are and the changes you're still making as a recovering person.

6. As you continue to relax into your breath, notice what you are feeling and thinking. At the same time, allow your heart to yearn for what you want in your future with your recovering partner.

7. Whenever you're ready, take a few more breaths and open your eyes.

Conclusion

As you launch more fully into your relationship with your recovering partner, now is a good time to stop and assess where you stand. I suggest that you revisit the Relationship Quiz you completed in chapter 1. If you have your answers from before, you can compare and see how your thoughts and feelings have evolved. Do the statements have a different meaning for you now that you have begun to experiment with the practices introduced throughout the book?

With continued practice, you will be able to protect yourself from emotional relapse and reap the benefits of self-discovery. You will experience increasingly predictable feelings of serenity. From this day forward, remember to stop and pat yourself on the back for each positive action you take, because these actions add up. Eventually you will find that you are no longer wasting precious time on regret, resentment, hurt, or self-criticalness. Keep the 12-step program's slogan

"One Day at a Time" in mind as you stay on your path of recovery and as you enjoy the relationship you've chosen to stay in with your recovering partner. Know that you have the freedom to make mistakes and to be perfectly imperfect on the journey. Isn't it a relief to have the chance to start fresh upon waking each day?

If you haven't already, you will come to see that by increasing your ability to cope with the ups and downs of life through the practice of mindfulness, honest self-expression, and never-ending curiosity, your life will be richer than you ever thought possible. Don't forget, practicing mindfulness doesn't just mean sitting on a cushion with your eyes closed, paying attention to your breath. It also means bringing yourself into the present, in each waking moment. It means being fully engaged in whatever you are doing—with no judgment about the thoughts, feelings, and sensations you are experiencing—as you stay on your personal path of recovery from codependency.

I think it is safe to say that as you continue to work hard on cherishing your life, you will find it easier to love the recovering partner whom you've chosen to commit to. Your willingness to breathe out fear and breathe in faith every day will make the cycles of togetherness and separation that occur over the course of your recovering relationship feel more natural and less threatening. With that, you can look forward to a future with your recovering partner that is filled with renewable moments of true intimate connection, arising from the foundation of hard-earned trust and security that you yourself have built. Let the joy begin!

Recommended Readings

Bernstein, G. 2011. *Spirit Junkie: A Radical Road to Self-Love and Miracles.* New York: Crown Publishing Group.

Black, C. 2002. *It Will Never Happen to Me: Growing Up With Addiction as Youngsters, Adolescents, Adults.* Center City, MN: Hazelden.

Chödrön, P. 2009. *Taking the Leap: Freeing Ourselves from Old Habits and Fears.* Boston, MA: Shambhala.

Duhigg, C. 2012. *The Power of Habit: Why We Do What We Do in Life and Business.* New York: Random House.

DuPont, R. 1997. *The Selfish Brain: Learning from Addiction.* Washington, DC: American Psychiatric.

Frederick, R. 2009. *Living Like You Mean It: Use the Wisdom and Power of Your Emotions to Get the Life You Really Want.* San Francisco, CA: Jossey-Bass.

Fromm, E. 1956. *The Art of Loving.* New York: Harper.

Goldstein, E. 2012. *The Now Effect: How This Moment Can Change the Rest of Your Life.* New York: Atria.

Griffin, K. 2004. *One Breath at a Time: Buddhism and the Twelve Steps*. Emmaus, PA: Rodale.

Hanson, R., and R. Mendius. 2009. *Buddha's Brain: The Practical Neuroscience of Happiness, Love, and Wisdom*. Oakland, CA: New Harbinger.

Jacobs-Stewart, T. 2010. *Mindfulness and the 12 Steps*. Center City, MN: Hazelden.

Kornfield, J. 1993. *A Path With Heart: A Guide Through the Perils and Promises of Spiritual Life*. New York: Bantam Books.

Nhat Hanh, Thich. 1987. *Being Peace*. Berkeley, CA: Parallax.

Pattakos, A. 2008. *Prisoners of Our Thoughts: Viktor Frankl's Principles for Discovering Meaning in Life and Work*. 2nd ed. San Francisco, CA: Berrett-Koehler.

Perel, E. 2006. *Mating in Captivity: Reconciling the Erotic and the Domestic*. New York: HarperCollins.

Real, T. 2007. *The New Rules of Marriage: What You Need to Know to Make Marriage Work*. New York: Random House.

Ryan, T. 2012. *A Mindful Nation: How a Simple Practice Can Help Us Reduce Stress, Improve Performance, and Recapture the American Spirit*. Carlsbad, CA: Hay House.

Salzberg, S. 1995. *Loving Kindness: The Revolutionary Art of Happiness*. Boston, MA: Shambhala.

Scaer, R. 2005. *The Trauma Spectrum: Hidden Wounds and Human Resiliency*. New York: W.W. Norton.

Tatkin, S. 2011. *Wired for Love: How Understanding Your Partner's Brain and Attachment Style Can Help You Defuse Conflict and Build a Secure Relationship*. Oakland, CA: New Harbinger.

Trungpa, C. 1970. *Meditation in Action*. Boston, MA: Shambala.

Warren, K. 2012. *Choose Joy: Because Happiness Isn't Enough.* Grand Rapids, MI: Revell.

Wegscheider-Cruse, S. 1989. *Another Chance: Hope and Health for the Alcoholic Family.* Palo Alto, CA: Science & Behavior Books.

Williams, L. 2011. *Radical Medicine: Cutting-Edge Natural Therapies That Treat the Root Causes of Disease,* Rochester, VT: Healing Arts Press.

Williams, M., J. Teasdale, Z. Segal, and J. Kabat-Zinn. 2007. *The Mindful Way Through Depression: Freeing Yourself from Chronic Unhappiness.* New York: Guilford.

References

Al-Anon Family Group Headquarters. 1992. *Courage to Change: One Day at a Time in Al-Anon*. Virginia Beach, VA: Al-Anon Family Group Headquarters.

Alcoholics Anonymous. 1989. *A Day at a Time: Daily Reflections for Recovering People*. Center City, MN: Hazelden.

Alcoholics Anonymous. 1990. *Daily Reflections: A Book of Reflections by A.A. Members for A.A. Members*. Alcoholics Anonymous World Services.

Alcoholics Anonymous. 2013. *The Big Book*, 4th ed. Alcoholics Anonymous World Services. www.aa.org/bigbookonline

Betty Ford Institute Consensus Panel. 2007. "What Is Recovery? A Working Definition from the Betty Ford Institute." *Journal of Substance Abuse Treatment* 33: 221–228.

Blum, K., E. P. Noble, P. J. Sheridan, A. Montgomery, T. Ritchie, P. Jagadeeswaran, H. Nogami, A. H. Briggs, and J. B. Cohn. 1990. "Allelic Association of Human Dopamine D2 Receptor Gene in Alcoholism." *Journal of the American Medical Association* 263(15): 2055–2060.

Boecker, H., T. Sprenger, M. E. Spilker, G. Henriksen, M. Koppenhoefer, K. J. Wagner, M. Valet, A. Berthele, T. R. Tolle. "The Runner's High: Opioidergic Mechanisms in the Human Brain." *Cerebral Cortex* 18(11): 2523–2531. doi:10.1093/cercor/bhn013

Carter, T. 1998. "The Effects of Spiritual Practices on Recovery from Substance Abuse." *Journal of Psychiatric and Mental Health Nursing* 5(5): 1365–2850. doi:10.1046/j.1365-2850.1998.00153.x

Davis, D., and J. Hayes. 2011. "What Are the Benefits of Mindfulness? A Practice Review of Psychotherapy-Related Research." *Psychotherapy* 48(2): 198–208. doi:10.1037/a0022062

De Angelis, T. 2008. "PTSD Treatments Grow in Evidence, Effectiveness." Monitor on Psychology 39(1): 40. Available at http://www.apa.org /monitor/jan08/ptsd.aspx

Hazan, C. and P. Shaver. 1987. "Romantic Love Conceptualized as an Attachment Process." *Journal of Personality and Social Psychology* 52(3): 511–524.

Heller, K., and R. Swindle. 1983. "Social Networks, Perceived Social Support and Coping with Stress." In *Preventive Psychology: Theory, Research and Practice*, edited by R. Felner, L. Jason, J. Moritsugu, and S. Farber, 87–103. New York: Pergamon Press.

Hölzel, B., J. Carmody, K. Evans, E. Hoge, J. Dusek, L. Morgan, R. Pitman, and S. Lazar. 2010. "Stress Reduction Correlates with Structural Changes in the Amygdala." *Social, Cognitive, and Affective Neuroscience* 5(1): 11–17. doi:10.1093/scan/nsp034

Hölzel, B., J. Carmody, M. Vangel, C. Congleton, S. Yerramsetti, T. Gard, and S. Lazar. 2011. "Mindfulness Practice Leads to Increases in Regional Brain Gray Matter Density." *Psychiatry Research: Neuroimaging* 191(1): 36–42. doi:10.1016/j.pscychresns.2010.08.006

Kabat-Zinn, J. 1990. *Full Catastrophe Living: Using the Wisdom of Your Body and Mind to Face Stress, Pain, and Illness*. New York: Random House.

Lazar, S., G. Bush, R. Gollub, G. Fricchione, G. Khalsa, and H. Benson. 2000. "Functional Brain Mapping of the Relaxation Response and Meditation." *Neuroreport* 11(7): 1581–1585. doi:10.1097/00001756 -200005150-00041

Montag, C., P. Kirsch, C. Sauer, S. Markett, M. Reuter. 2012. "The Role of the CHRNA4 Gene in Internet Addiction: A Case-Control Study." *Journal of Addiction Medicine* 6(3): 191–195. doi:10.1097/ADM.0b013 e31825ba7e7

Shapiro, F. 1995. *Eye Movement Desensitization and Reprocessing: Basic Principles, Protocols and Procedures*. New York: Guilford Press.

Beverly Berg, MFT, PhD, is a therapist and author whose work has been founded on cutting-edge therapies such as eye movement desensitization and reprocessing (EMDR); emotional freedom techniques (EFT); and the indirect hypnosis methods of Milton H. Erickson, which integrate psychological, emotional, physical, and spiritual well-being, and focus on the complex relationship between the body and the mind.

Photograph by Brian Wry

Foreword writer **Stan Tatkin, PsyD, MFT,** is a clinician, researcher, teacher, and developer of the psychobiological approach to couples therapy. He teaches and supervises family medicine residents at Kaiser Permanente in Woodland Hills and lives with his wife and daughter in Calabasas, CA.